"Ask The Expert"

As heard on KMOX Radio

Tony La Russa Talks Baseball Strategy
With Joe Buck

All proceeds to Dollar-Help, Inc.

COVER PHOTO: Taken by photographer Todd Anderson

Photograph courtesy of
The Sporting News, 10176 Corporate Square Drive, Suite 200,
St. Louis, MO 63132-2294

© 2002 Dollar-Help, Inc.

All rights reserved. No part of this book may be reproduced or tranmitted in any form, by any means (eletronic, photocopying, recording or otherwise, whether now known or hereafter invented) without the prior written permission of Dollar-Help, Inc.

ISBN 0-9710910-0-5

FORWARD

Each year since 1996, generally on the open date after Opening Day, I have attended a seminar on baseball strategy conducted by one of the masters, Cardinals' Manager Tony La Russa. Fortunately for Cardinal fans, Laclede Gas and KMOX Radio have had these seminars recorded, and portions are broadcast prior to each game as part of the "Laclede Gas Ask The Expert" series. Now, all baseball fans have the opportunity to participate in an extended seminar by reading this book, which is a compilation of Tony's answers to more than 300 questions about why a major league manager makes the decisions he does.

Second-guessing the manager is as much a part of baseball as the boxscore. Tony acknowledges that there are several ways to do things and "strategy" is just one man's opinion. But as you read this book, you'll find, as I did, that his opinions are particularly well informed and highly analytical. Yet his decisions on the field have to be made in an instant. The move either works or it doesn't, but it has to be made right then.

Similarly, Tony's answers that you'll read here were made in an instant. He never saw a single question ahead of time, and the people at Laclede Gas put together very good questions about situations managers face every day. No softballs here. But, with the tape rolling and only 85 seconds to answer, Tony consistently hit it dead on. A lot of major league managers react to these situations, but I don't know how many put as much thought into their decisions or could explain their thinking so coherently on a moment's notice.

As you read Tony's answers, I think you'll be as amazed as I am at how deeply he thinks about game situations and how many alternatives race through his mind. Tony La Russa is a terrific baseball man who carries inside him a deep love and respect for the game and the people who taught it to him. In this book, he shares all that and more.

I have been fortunate to be a part of this series, as I consider it a great learning experience. So will any fan who loves the game or wants to learn more about how it really works.

Joe Buck
March 2002

About Dollar-Help

Dollar-Help is a not-for-profit crisis intervention program that helps the poorest of the poor in St. Louis and southeastern Missouri pay their heating bills. The typical recipient of Dollar-Help assistance is a low-income, elderly or disabled person with an annual household income of less than $6,500.

Dollar-Help assistance helps pay heating bills of any type — natural gas, electric, heating oil and propane — and is only made available after the recipient has exhausted all avenues of public funds for energy assistance.

Since its inception in 1982, Dollar-Help, Inc., has raised and distributed more than $9 million to needy families. All contributions go entirely to help people in need. There are no administrative costs taken out of the contributions because the Board of Directors of Dollar-Help, Inc., consists entirely of community leaders who serve without compensation, Laclede Gas Company provides fund-raising, administrative and support services, while several social service organizations in eastern Missouri and numerous energy vendors also volunteer their assistance.

In keeping with the concept of Dollar-Help, all proceeds from the purchase of this book will go directly to help someone keep warm in the winter.

If you would like to learn more about Dollar-Help, check our website at www.dollarhelp.org. If you would like to make a further contribution to Dollar-Help, you can do so in several ways: **1)** Check the red box on your Laclede Gas bill to have a $1 contribution automatically added to your monthly gas bills; **2)** Call or write Laclede Gas to have a regular contribution of any amount you specify included on your Laclede Gas bill; **3)** Overpay your Laclede Gas bill by exactly $1; **4)** Make a bequest in your Last Will and Testament; **5)** Mail a contribution to the Dollar-Help fund at Cass Bank, P.O. Box 330, St. Louis, MO 63166.

All contributions to Dollar-Help are tax-deductible. Dollar-Help's most recent Annual Report, including its audited financial statement, is available for viewing on the website.

www.dollarhelp.org

Table of Contents

Chapter One – Team Management 7

Chapter Two – Lineups 48

Chapter Three – Game Decisions 64

Chapter Four – Offense. 112

Chapter Five – Base Running 133

Chapter Six – Defense. 143

Chapter Seven – Pitching 164

Chapter Eight – Statistics 185

Chapter Nine – Miscellaneous. 189

Tony La Russa and Joe Buck Biography 221

Acknowledgements. 222

About the Laclede Gas "Ask The Expert" series on KMOX

The Laclede Gas "Ask The Expert" series was begun in 1996 as an advertising campaign linking the natural gas experts in St. Louis (Laclede Gas) with the St. Louis Cardinals' resident baseball expert (Manager Tony La Russa), and is given further luster by the participation of one of broadcasting's best talents, Joe Buck. Individual questions and answers are aired on KMOX Radio during the Cardinals' pre-game show.

Laclede Gas Company is proud to be associated with Tony, Joe, KMOX and the Cardinals in producing what has become part of the regular flow of inside information expected by baseball's best and most knowledgeable fans.

Laclede and KMOX also have teamed in other ways to raise funds for Dollar-Help, a vital heating assistance program that helps the poorest of poor keep warm in winter. The compilation of six seasons worth of "Ask The Expert" questions and answers into a book for sale to benefit Dollar-Help seemed a natural extension of this partnership.

Laclede Gas Company is the largest natural gas distribution utility in Missouri, serving more than 630,000 residential, commercial and industrial customers in St. Louis and surrounding counties of eastern Missouri. It is the primary subsidiary of The Laclede Group, Inc. (NYSE: LG), a public holding company committed to providing reliable natural gas service through its regulated core utility operations while developing its presence in non-regulated activities that fit well and provide opportunities for sustainable growth.

KMOX Radio — News/Talk 1120 — has been the broadcast home of St. Louis Cardinals' baseball for nearly 50 years, serving as the flagship station for a network that now includes more than 100 stations covering 11 states. Since its beginning in 1925, 1925, KMOX has brought informative, innovative talk radio to the region and the nation. KMOX proudly continues to hold the distinct honor of being the most dominant radio station in the history of broadcasting in America, with a record 103 consecutive number one showings in the Arbitron ratings.

TEAM MANAGEMENT

JOE BUCK: Does a team approach a road game any differently from the way it prepares for a home game?

TONY LA RUSSA: That's a good question, and I know a very appropriate one for the Cardinals, because they had such a tough time winning on the road last year. I think there are a few things you do differently. At home, sometimes teams are tailored to their home ball park, and when you go on the road, you feel you're at a disadvantage because maybe you're built for speed and this is a power park, or vice versa. We try to convince our players we're building a well-balanced team that can win in any situation regardless of the weather and type of ballpark. What you think about on the road is: You're going to go on the road and show off. That's an attitude that I'd like to instill on our ball club. Fans in the visiting city are only going to get to see our club twice a year, so we're really going to have them remember St. Louis Cardinal baseball. The other important thing is: Relief pitching is very important on the road. Normally, if you get deep into a ballgame — extra innings, for example — the advantage really goes to the home club, so you want to be able to have strong relief pitching if you're going to be successful on the road as well as have a well-balanced club.

JOE BUCK: Okay Tony La Russa, here's today's question. Why do ball clubs often look flat the first home game after a long road trip?

TONY LA RUSSA: Well, that's a truism. That's a good question, because if you watch ball clubs very often, it's not just the change of scenery. I think, physically, there's a carryover as far as the fatigue and the stress you go through on the road. It catches up with you. In fact, some people even believe that, on the second day, you feel worse than the first day after a real stressful or physically and mentally taxing trip. One of the things we try to do is change the routine the day we come back. I know when I was in Oakland and we were coming from the East Coast to the West Coast, we had a quite a problem with that. What you do

TEAM MANAGEMENT

sometimes is: On that first day you don't have batting practice. You want to make a point to the team that we're going to save every bit of energy we have for the ballgame, and we're not going to waste it on practice. I think it makes you a little fresher, and it makes a point to the team — "Hey, you know if we're not careful, we can come out there and be listless, so let's make sure we save every bit of effort for the ballgame."

JOE BUCK: Okay Tony, here's today's question. Can you teach fundamentals at the big league level, or is it impossible to change bad habits at this time in the good ones?

TONY LA RUSSA: That's a very important area for baseball in the '90s. There is such a priority now in rushing young pitchers and players to the big leagues, very often you will have a player come to the big leagues and he'll have something technically wrong with his game. I don't think it's unusual; it's more usual. That's why there's so much teaching that goes on at the big league level as opposed to years ago when there were so many more minor leagues, and you had to work your way up. If it's a fundamental, to me a fundamental means it's something that's very basic to the game, and you ought to be able to repeat it automatically if you do the right thing over and over and over again. When you get in the game, you're not thinking, "Well if I bunt, I've got to get my bat out in front of the plate; I've got to have that certain angle." All those fundamentals, if you're willing to go through repetition and you're repeating the right way to do it over and over again, you'll build automatically. So yes, you can change bad fundamentals, but it takes a lot of work, and it still goes on every day at the big league level all over baseball.

TEAM MANAGEMENT

JOE BUCK: Okay Tony La Russa, here's today's question. It's a fact that as a player ages his physical skills will tend to diminish, but how much can a player compensate for the loss of physical ability by experience in this game of baseball?

TONY LA RUSSA: Well, that's a tremendous asset. In fact, there's an old saying that experience is a great equalizer. I think the important first point to make is that, nowadays, with the advances in physical conditioning, you're seeing these outstanding athletes get on fitness programs that keep those abilities alive. In our ball club, we've got guys in their 30s and 40s who are still competing very well, and they're really using that part of it. As you start to lose something off your fastball; if you lose a little bit of speed on the bases; if you're a hitter and you don't have quite the same power — the fact you've got all this experience, that you really understand what hitting and pitching and base running is about, it helps you continue to succeed at a high level. For example, a pitcher like Tom Seaver. I can remember I saw him toward the end of his career when he no longer had that 90-plus fastball. He really relied on excellent command and changing speeds, so you always learn what makes you successful. Things you were told as a young hitter or pitcher that you really don't understand — once you start playing four, five, six hundred games, they start to make sense about the time you start to recede a little physically. Then the experience picks up, and you can still compete.

JOE BUCK: Do you believe games are won or lost by managerial decisions?

TONY LA RUSSA: I've heard that question answered many different ways. My version is: I don't believe managers ever win the games, but the players do. I think managers can lose games, though. You think about what a manager is supposed to do for a ball club. You're supposed to make certain decisions as far as strategy, as far as setting lineups, and as far as making pitching changes, that put the players in the best position to be successful. If you don't do a good job of that, you can really contribute to

TEAM MANAGEMENT

losing. I think the other thing a manager is supposed to do is: He's supposed to get a club fired up and excited about trying to play hard and win games. If you're a guy who the club doesn't respond to and the club is lackadaisical, then I think you can really contribute to losing. I think winning players are the ones who go out there and put their necks on the line, but if a manager is not doing his job, then it can contribute to losing.

JOE BUCK: Okay Tony La Russa, here is today's question. Besides giving them as much playing time as possible, how can a manager make reserves feel like important parts of the ball club?

TONY LA RUSSA: The key thing is: How much actual playing time can you give them? I think everybody understands if you have a couple of hitters who are your main pinch-hitters, occasionally they have to have a full game when they get 4 or 5 at bats. The things you do during the game are really the most important. I have also found that if you pay a lot of attention to the workouts before the game, then you can tell the guys who are your non-starters that day to be sure they get a good physical day out there, and they really work all of their techniques. You can get kind of lazy and take for granted different pieces of the game, so we really work hard for our extra men to do something with their arms, with their legs, with their defensive ability, and to make sure they get enough swings. The other thing you can do — and it's a status thing — is you can be sure you treat them like stars in the clubhouse and when you're traveling. You don't treat them like some kind of second-class citizens.

JOE BUCK: Okay Tony La Russa, here is today's question. Can an off day actually be bad for a hot team's momentum?

TONY LA RUSSA: Truthfully, there are times when you are playing well, and you get that off day, you don't want it but it's one of the givens when you start the season. You're going to look at the

TEAM MANAGEMENT

schedule, and there are going to be days off. What you don't want your club to do is get psycho about something like, "Oh, we're really hot, and now we have a day off." I think you always try to search for the positive so you can point out to the ball club that they have been working so hard, and if they can just catch their breath on the off day, they'll be even better the day after the off day. Another P.S. to that is something we learned. Many times, on the day after an off day, players are very sluggish and the teams are slow to get back into the groove of playing. It may be the 4th or 5th inning before they feel comfortable and their timing is right. We've always had this saying on ball clubs where, on the day after the off day, during the practice we are all pushing each other. You have to push early so you can start feeling competitive from the first pitch because it is not going to happen automatically. The off day takes a little edge away from you.

JOE BUCK: Okay Tony, here is today's question. When the wind is blowing straight out at Wrigley Field, and everyone has visions of home run after home run after home run, how do you control your guys and not allow them to just go up there and pump for the fences?

TONY LA RUSSA: I don't like the word "control." That is not how you create an atmosphere on a ball club. What you try to do is coach. You try to explain, persuade and teach. The key word is "discipline." Any good hitter is a disciplined hitter. To me, there are at least a couple of meanings there. One of them is that you don't swing at everything the pitcher throws up there. You have to have a certain discipline in the strike zone, and you want to be aggressive with the pitches you can handle. Secondly, and this is the point of this question, you want to have the discipline that you put on your best stroke where you are trying to make hard contact. It is a natural tendency, when you have the wind blowing out or you are playing in a small bandbox-type ballpark, for hitters to want to hit the cheap home run. When does that happen? When they get the count in their favor — 1 and 0, 2 and 0, or 2 and 1. They see that fastball, their eyes light up, and they try to lift the ball

TEAM MANAGEMENT

out of the park. What usually happens is: They pop it up or they miss. What you try to teach is that good hitters will take advantage of conditions, such as the wind blowing out in Wrigley, by just trying to hit the ball hard. What you end up having is some line drive base hits, and then if you catch it a little fuller you will hit a home run. If you try to hit a home run with your lift swing, you're just going to pop it up or miss it.

JOE BUCK: Okay Tony, here is today's question. Why do teams tend to rest so many regulars on Sunday instead of spacing out the rest during the week, and then on Sunday you get the team of bench players. Why don't you spread it out and let guys rest during the week?

TONY LA RUSSA: Actually, I agree it's a better thing to do. I think it's better to spread the rest throughout the week. You don't want to make Sunday the junior varsity game or anything. The other thing I think makes a lot of sense is: You want to spot players off your bench in with a bunch of regulars. If you can give a regular a game off, and you play an irregular guy and you do that throughout the week, then you don't have 4 or 5 players, the nucleus of your ball club, sitting and watching the game. One reason I think you see that done quite a bit in the big leagues is that there are so many games played on Saturday night that, at the end of a tough week, the Sunday day game gets there so quickly after the Saturday night game. Usually, in the middle of the summer when it gets hotter, managers will go with the philosophy of fresh legs and fresh blood. That means you're better off with a rested player than with a guy who is fatigued, even though he's one of your stars. I think it's better to spread the bench out throughout the series, but I do think on Sunday afternoon you will have to rest a player or two because that day game gets there in a hurry.

TEAM MANAGEMENT

JOE BUCK: Okay Tony, here's today's question. How can a manager and his players maintain a positive outlook during a losing streak, and how can they avoid getting too high during a winning streak?

TONY LA RUSSA: That's one of those cases where leadership is so important, and the veterans on your ball club can really take charge. For example, if you're having a tough time and the younger players tend to droop or get depressed because they think this is the end of the world, the veterans can tell them, "Hey it's a 162-game season; you're playing for six months. Once in a while this happens, and all you really have to do is concentrate on winning the next game you play." Don't think about the four or five you just got beat; just concentrate on today but understand the worm is going to turn and the breaks will start coming your way as long as you stay positive and upbeat. It's the same thing if you start playing well. Sometimes the younger players will get very excited. They'll think, "This is the greatest life anybody could ever live; you're in the big leagues, you're winning, you're doing great." And you start getting so giddy that, when the game slaps you and humbles you, it's a long way back down. That inconsistency will drive you nuts, and you're not a good club. Leadership, coaches, and veteran players can tone the young guys down when you're going well by telling them to just feel good about it but always keep looking for that next success. Major League baseball is geared to the next success, not your last one.

JOE BUCK: Some teams seem to be much better than others at fundamentals, like throwing to the right base, hitting the cutoff man, hitting behind the runner and so on. How do you make sure your teams are fundamentally sound?

TONY LA RUSSA: It's a very important area and I think it's a special responsibility of the manager and the coaches. I think there are a couple of ways you should judge a team and directly hold the staff responsible, especially the manager. One of them is the effort the team gives, and another one is on the fundamentals. It's your

TEAM MANAGEMENT

responsibility as a manager to convince the players that these fundamental plays — which are, more than anything else, plays that are repeated over and over again — if you practice them so they're memorized and can be repeated in game conditions, they're directly instrumental in whether you win or lose games. That's a part of your responsibility, and the piece I just talked about is how you acquire that skill. You have to practice it over and over again. You have to be willing, as a manager or coach, to point out to somebody when they make a mistake. If you miss a cutoff man or if you do something wrong, you have to make a point to say, 'That's not the way we play the game.' It's a true statement: The best team doesn't always win. It's the team who plays the best. So your objective is to play the best baseball.

JOE BUCK: Okay Tony La Russa, here is today's question. Is it necessary to have at least 1 or 2 so-called junk-ballers on a pitching staff?

TONY LA RUSSA: Actually, it does present a real advantage to a ball club when you have some off-speed pitchers who can be in your rotation as well as your bullpen. I say that because there's a real plus in having contrasting styles with your pitching staff. I can remember Baltimore in the '70s. They had 5 starters, and they were all different, with Mike Cuellar, Dave McNally, and Jim Palmer. Every time you faced their pitching staff, the hitter had to make an adjustment. If you have a lot of the same looking pitchers over the course of a 3- or 4-game series, then in the second, third or fourth game the hitters will start to get on a speed or a type of fastball or slider. That's why you don't like to have all power or all junk balls. The complement is very good when you can throw them off balance by mixing in somebody who throws very hard with somebody who has good command of off-speed stuff.

TEAM MANAGEMENT

JOE BUCK: Okay Tony La Russa, here's today's question. When an organization assembles a pitching staff, how much emphasis does it put on the proportion of left-handers versus right-handed pitching?

TONY LA RUSSA: I think the answer to that is, first of all, are you talking about starting pitchers or are you talking about your bullpen? If you're talking about starting pitchers, what you need to do is assemble the five best starting pitchers, whether they're five left-handers or five right-handers. It's beautiful to have a balance where you had, for example three rights and two lefts. That is very nice, but in today's baseball with pitching being such a priority, you just can't fill in the rotation the way you would like to. You need to pick the best players. I think with the starting rotation, if you had balance that's fine, but just pick the best guys. On the other hand, I think it's very important in your bullpen to have at least a couple of left-hand weapons. I think the perfect bullpen would be something such as three guys each way so you really could have the advantage going into every series of attacking the other manager's lineup early, middle, and late in the game.

JOE BUCK: What mix do you like to see in the bullpen? Is there an ideal mix such as so many right-handers or so many left-handers, power pitchers, control guys, what do you like?

TONY LA RUSSA: I think a flexible bullpen is one of the biggest keys to success now. By that, I mean flexibility in terms of if they are right-handed or left-handed. Do you have somebody primarily who can get you those three outs in the ninth inning? That is the lynch pin in your bullpen. However, for all of the important outs before that, you need set-up guys, and they have to be a variety. Teams differ. You may have a very strong right-hand lineup, like last years Montreal Expos, for example. They were very strong right-handed, and then they had the one left-hander here or there, like Henry Rodriguez. You want the specialist left-hander to come in and do that. You may have some time in games where both pitchers are giving up runs, so you have to pitch a lot of innings

TEAM MANAGEMENT

with your bullpen. In your bullpen, you want to have the flexibility to have an innings guy, somebody that can go out there and give you two or three innings, where he holds the other team down. So for me, it's a combination of lefts and rights, players who can pitch to one or two hitters versus one or two innings, and if they can complement their stuff. If you've got a pitcher who has a sinkerball, some pitcher who cuts fastballs, some pitcher who is a high-rider pitcher, and some pitcher who even has a knuckle ball, all of that can be mysterious to the other side.

JOE BUCK: You've got a player with one of those nagging day-to-day injuries. A key situation arises in which he would be the perfect player. Would you use him or keep him on the bench in case you wanted to put him on the DL retroactively?

TONY LA RUSSA: My assumption is that, if a player is on the active roster, he can be used that day to win a game. I think it's too much to comprehend as a manager whether, if I use him, that uses one more day of his disabled time. You make a judgment as an organization, from the general manager to the trainer, to the coaching staff on player availability. Then the only reason you wouldn't use him is, "Am I going to aggravate that injury and prevent him from playing two or three days from now, or am I better off not using him and resting him?" For example, if you have a guy with a hamstring problem, and he's out for a day or two, you probably don't want to pinch-hit him with the bases loaded and one out. If it's a ground ball, he's going to try to beat it out, and sure enough, he's going to blow that hamstring again. So you look for a two-out situation where, if he doesn't get a base hit to produce a run, he can just limp over to first base and doesn't have to feel like he has to be a hero. The idea is: If the guy's available, you use him and try to be careful, but you don't worry about the disabled list.

TEAM MANAGEMENT

JOE BUCK: Tony, a young player coming up in September may be over-awed or over-matched. How do you evaluate whom you call up in September?

TONY LA RUSSA: I think you have to be very careful. Number one, adding people to your roster depends on your situation. If you've got a club in contention, you don't want to populate your clubhouse with a lot of people. You might tend to distract the club from trying to finish off an outstanding season. You want to be very careful. Everyone you call up should only be there to help you win a game. However, if you're having a tough season, you may have other purposes. You may want to expose some guys to the big leagues and get their feet wet so they can get an idea what the big leagues look like. They'll be impressed if their ability matches up well. One thing you'll want to evaluate though, and be careful with a September call-up: The pressure's off if you're losing, and if you're winning, you're not going to play them very much. Don't get too carried away with what happens in September. Very rarely does a guy play enough or make enough of an impression where that particular opportunity creates enough in your mind to say, "We're going to go with this guy in the upcoming season." September has its value, but be very careful. Don't get too carried away with a guy who struggles or does very well. It isn't as meaningful as a full six-month season.

JOE BUCK: When you call a rookie up from the minor leagues to the majors, he has to be nervous. Is it best to get him right into the game, or do you let him sit for awhile and get acclimated to the big leagues?

TONY LA RUSSA: I think the first thing you do is talk to him. You tell him, "If you're not nervous, that means you're not ready." You try to get him to accept the fact that the jitters and the anxiety are an important part of being successful. If he ever starts to lose that, he's getting too comfortable. I think the specific answer to the question, in my opinion, is that you try to play him as soon as you possibly can. Normally, you promote a pitcher or a hitter because

TEAM MANAGEMENT

he's performing well in Triple A, so he comes up with some confidence about how he is going to pitch or hit. If he has to sit around and wait, what do you think he's going to do during that time? He's going to think, he's going to worry, and pretty soon he's going to lose that naturalness or confidence he came up with. As often as you can, try to bring him up and use him. I think that's always one of the little games you play as far as being a manager. You bring up a player, and maybe the team is going well so he's just going to be protection at some position. You don't want to disrupt what's going well just to take care of one guy. You always try to do what's best for the team; it's nice when it works out — what's best for the individual is best for the team. Normally you try to play him right away, but only if it's best for the team.

JOE BUCK: Tony, some managers have a lefty in the bullpen whose main job is to face just one tough left-handed batter in the game. Others let pitchers face however many hitters they can. How do you feel about carrying a so-called one-out left-hander?

TONY LA RUSSA: I do think that's one of the specialists who is worth putting on your club and using up a roster space. There are so many dangerous left-hand hitters in the league that, if you have a left-hand pitcher who's devastating against a left-hand hitter, he's worth it. That's one of the advantages I had for years and years with Rick Honeycutt. It's great if you have a left-hander who could really wipe-out the great left-hand hitter, but also could be used against right-handers because he had pitches to retire them as well. Still, if this guy is only effective against left-handers, and the key guy coming to bat is a tough left-hander like Barry Bonds or Fred McGriff, what you're looking for is a left-hander who can wipe them out. It's worth having that guy on your roster just to get you that one out, and then you'll go to your other options. There are times when you'll have that left-hand pitcher who's he really is vulnerable against right-hand hitters — maybe he's a side-arm — but he is worth having on your staff if you can find him.

TEAM MANAGEMENT

JOE BUCK: Tony, when rainouts and off days occur, do you bump the fifth starter to keep your first four in rotation? And if you do that, how do you keep your fifth starter in shape and game ready?

TONY LA RUSSA: It really depends on your pitching staff. Most staffs struggle to have four good starters, so your classic situation is that the fifth guy is your swingman. It's more important, and I think most baseball people would tell you this, to keep your starters working regularly. So you're better off bumping the one guy and having the other four guys stay as close to regular as possible, working every fifth day. That has the advantage of bolstering your bullpen. When you do that, you put your fifth guy into the pen, and it gives you that extra reliever. I've had some success with that over the years. I remember I had Jerry Koosman and Dennis Lamp when we were with the White Sox, and they were devastating in that role. They would take the occasional start and still be very effective. However, if you have a deep staff, sometimes it makes more sense to go ahead and keep all five guys working. If you plan to have five guys effective in pitching a lot, you go ahead and give the extra rest. You sometimes look at later in the season, when a pitcher's arm starts hanging a little bit, and he can use that extra day or two of rest. So it's really a judgment call.

JOE BUCK: Tony, Casey Stengel used to juggle his rotation so Whitey Ford would pitch most of the time against the better clubs. Do you let your rotation fall however it may, or do you try to match your best pitchers against the stronger teams?

TONY LA RUSSA: This is one of those questions you'll get arguments about among baseball people. For example, if you're thinking about piling up a number of wins, you can get your Whitey Ford against a weaker team and have more of a guarantee of getting that win. If you're going to win ball games, it doesn't matter what team you win them against, as long as you pile up that right total. The other argument, though, is if you're going to play against the better team, to be successful over the course of the season,

TEAM MANAGEMENT

you're going to have to compete against those guys. So you have to stick your aces on those best clubs. You can argue both ways. I think what usually happens, if you keep messing with your rotation to get the match ups in your favor, as far as your aces pitching against the better team, you'll disrupt your rotation so much that it will end up hurting you more than helping you. Most pitchers like the habit and the routine of pitching every fifth day. Occasionally, I think you can use an off day where you can stretch a player for a couple of days or pitch a guy one day short of rest if you want to create that match-up against the tough club, but usually you don't mess with it.

JOE BUCK: In 1994, Tony, Felipe Alou had no left-handers in his bullpen, yet his Expos finished with the best record in the league. How important to you is that righty-lefty balance in the bullpen?

TONY LA RUSSA: Another recent example is when the Cardinals played the Padres in 1996, and that's a club that won the Western Division. The Padres had no left-hander in their bullpen. I think that's one of the things when you put a club together, there's a certain, perfect formula you look for as far as the infielder-outfielder protection, the catcher and all this left-right platoon you're catching. There's no doubt, I think, in anyone's mind that, if you had your preference, you would like to have a couple of lefts — some people like three lefts and three rights as the perfect way, or at least four and two. However, it's so important to have a left-hander to neutralize that tough left-hand hitter, that if you find one, I've seen clubs win with one left-hander. To go without one, I think it's a terrific disadvantage. It means that any time you go against a club, especially if you have a right-hand rotation, they can stack all their left-handers against you and not ever worry about the manager on the other side coming back with a left-hander to neutralize them. So I definitely believe this is one of those parts of the formula you have to really work at, to get some left-right balance in your bullpen. If you don't, you make the best of it. You just hope your right-handers can get left-hand hitters out.

TEAM MANAGEMENT

JOE BUCK: **Tony, some teams carry three catchers on their 25-man roster, while others get by with only two. What goes into the decision to keep a third catcher instead of an extra pitcher or an extra position player in reserve?**

TONY LA RUSSA: Most times the third catcher has to have some versatility beyond catching. I don't think many clubs can afford to have three guys who are primarily catchers. What you often have are two guys who will split the duty. The third guy can get back there if the game dictates, but he has other abilities. With the Cardinals, a Danny Sheaffer is so versatile; he can play third, he can play the outfield, and he's a very good pinch-hitter. Normally going with two catchers, which a lot of clubs get into and I've done it myself, allows you the luxury of maybe protecting your pitching staff with another pitcher. However, then you've got to look at your catchers. If you have catchers who, when they start, they're good hitters and they run pretty well. You don't have to worry about pinch-hitting or pinch-running, because usually that second catcher sitting there is enough protection. On our club, with Tom Pagnozzi, if you get into a late-game situation where he gets on base, you're going to have to run for him. You run for him, and your second catcher goes in, you play late in the game, and you have no protection. It's very dangerous to go with two.

JOE BUCK: **Tony, do you ever play a player out of position just to get a look at how he might do there in the future?**

TONY LA RUSSA: In spring training you do it all the time. Hopefully, during the season, you don't have too many games where you're not concerned about winning, or maybe you're out of contention and you start building for the future. I think that's really the best answer. If you get to the last month of the season and you're out of it, it's smart to try to look ahead. For example, a player can be somebody like John Mabry as a third baseman. It wouldn't have been bad to try to play him at third to get an idea. However, I think in the championship season, when you've got something on the line, experimenting is the wrong way to go about

TEAM MANAGEMENT

it. What does happen, though, because of the demands of a championship season on a roster, you can get depleted for a particular game or series, and you may see a player play out of position, but it's because of necessity. You can't call up somebody from the minor leagues that will be better than what you have. I can remember we played a game against Cleveland last year. Danny Shaeffer ended up at second base in one of the inter-league games. If it's a necessity, you have to do it, but I wouldn't do it just to evaluate unless you are out of the race.

JOE BUCK: **Tony, why aren't pitchers used more as pinch-runners? Wouldn't that avoid depleting your bench?**

TONY LA RUSSA: Yes, it would. But I think the risk factor is so critical there that it's not worth the gamble, unless you're talking about late in the game and you really have a short bench, or when you started out the day, whether your bench was a little shorter because of injuries, or the way the first half of the game was played, you used up a couple of extra players. There's a general rule: With pitchers on the bases, you're asking for trouble. These guys are all good competitors. What they'll try to do is break up a double play. They don't really slide a lot. They're not involved in that offensive part of the game. You might have somebody land on his wrist, or they might get kicked. They might just have a hamstring pull, because you're talking usually about starters between their starts. They've had a full workday of preparation with their legs, their midsections and their arms, and now they're sitting back there kind of cool and kind of tight. You put this player into the heat of the battle, and you're likely to have some type of pull, if not some type of break. So, I think it really is a dumb move. I don't care how fast a guy is; he is only to be used in an emergency late in the game when you really do have a short bench.

TEAM MANAGEMENT

JOE BUCK: Tony, when putting together your bench, how many infielders, outfielders and so forth do you like to keep?

TONY LA RUSSA: I think the general rule is you want at least a couple infielders and a couple of outfielders. I think the real key — especially in the National League you hear about this all the time, but you can obviously see it — the more versatile a player is, the more that player can play the infield and the outfield. If one player can play the infield and catch or the outfield and catch, then that player has extra value to your ball club. I think what you end up doing: You start putting your roster together. You go for your key guys, what you have as the nucleus of your club. Then you start building around that. As you start finishing out your roster, then you'll start to see, "Hey, wait a minute, our key guys are all right-handed!" Then you try to get some left-hand balance. Or we're very fast but we don't have much power, so you want to finish out your club with some power. It goes beyond just whether is he an infielder or an outfielder. You look for versatility, and more than anything else you look for complements to the nucleus of your club. In the end, the better balance you have, the more you can compete over six months in all the different competitive situations that a major league club faces.

JOE BUCK: Tony, when you look down at your bench, do you prefer to see veterans or youngsters who are gaining experience?

TONY LA RUSSA: I think here the general rule is one that I agree with. Most baseball people will tell you that the bench should be made up of players with experience. One of the toughest burdens you can put on a young player is to bring him into the big leagues and sit him on the bench. Most young players need the daily activity to refine their skills, to keep their timing, and to improve their game. You put a young player on the bench, he's not sure of his playing time, he's going to get a pinch-hit here or there, an occasional start, and they end up going backward rather than forward. You get a veteran who's been around a long time, he

TEAM MANAGEMENT

understands the game. He has a much better idea what he needs to do to get ready. Willie McGee is the perfect example. He knows his work routine. He knows what to do to get ready for that spot in the seventh or eighth. He has a wealth of experience to call on to deal with a certain situation. So for me, the bench players should be veterans, and now you put young guys in for economics. The opposite is true in the bullpen. There's nothing wrong with having a young pitcher develop out of the bullpen to start getting some experience. So I think: Young, better in the bullpen, and veterans, better off the bench.

JOE BUCK: Tony, what do you do to make sure your bench players play enough to stay sharp?

TONY LA RUSSA: This is one of the real problems for a manager throughout the season and a much bigger problem in the American League. This is because, in the American League with that DH, especially if your club is built around a legitimate DH, the bench player doesn't get in the game automatically. In the National League with the pitcher in the lineup, it's much easier to at least give some playing time to your bench players. However, I think there are two different philosophies here. One is that you play the eight guys every day, and the bench guys are there for emergencies, and every once in a while you see a club win that way. But if you look at ball clubs that win most of the time, they really involve the whole roster. What you try to do with your bench players is: You try to understand that they're going to be called on during the course of the season to make a play or get a base hit. You've got to give them enough playing time where their timing is alive and well. So what does that mean? That means you should give them a game every week or so where they get their four at bats. It also has the twin benefit that, every day a bench player plays, one of your nucleus guys sits. Over a six-month season, if you can rest that nucleus guy once in a great while, it really has a way to refresh him. So you pick up the best of both worlds.

TEAM MANAGEMENT

JOE BUCK: Tony, it might be several days between games for a utility player. How does he stay prepared for his role as a pinch-hitter or a defensive replacement?

TONY LA RUSSA: He stays prepared with work, a lot of work. I think, as a manager, one thing to do is give him a lot attention. With some of the best managers I've been around, they make sure their extra guys get talked to everyday. They make sure they know that their role is important, and they have a responsibility. You just don't talk to the stars and ignore your extra guy, because he's going to be called upon during the course of the season to do something important. However, the bottom line is work. Now, he's going to get into the game, he's going to sit there, and it's very good — when the day is over — even if he didn't contribute to that game, to know he did something productive. You want to make sure he does a lot of work with his legs. Infielder or outfielder, depending on what it is, you want to make sure he does a lot of technique work, takes a lot of ground balls and takes a lot of fly balls. You want to give him as much hitting as you can. We have different hitting drills we can give an extra player on a day he doesn't play. He can go in the cage. We can give him extra hitting. We can give him situations almost like he was actually playing in a game. The bottom line, I think, that you want to really stress is to make sure, conditioning-wise, a guy is really working so his body is alive and fresh, and he doesn't go backward in his conditioning just sitting around. You also want to talk to him and make sure he knows how important he is.

TEAM MANAGEMENT

JOE BUCK: Tony, in the '80s the Cardinals won with good pitching, great defense, contact hitters and aggressive base running. Today in baseball, that style seems to have been abandoned and teams are trying to outslug each other. Why is that the case? And was that the style of play you envisioned as you and Walt Jocketty built the roster?

TONY LA RUSSA: You always start with the type of personnel that you have. When we came into this situation, Walt was here a year or two before I was here, and we had some players who already had some extra-base pop. The nice thing about some of the guys who were here, and I'm thinking about guys like Ray Lankford or Brian Jordan, was because they had extra-base pop, it didn't mean they had to sacrifice good defense and good base running. I think the issue about slugging versus contact guys who run the bases is more prevalent in the American League, where the style is slug, slug, slug, because you have the DH and because you have hitter-friendly ballparks. You usually try to build a ball club that has more chances for multiple run innings. In the National League, a lot of games are played where it's very important to make a run or stop a run. For that, you need a club that can have a lot of different weapons: Able to run the bases, able to execute the little things, and able to play good defense. With the Cardinals, we're trying to win all types of games, the high-scoring ones and the low-scoring ones.

JOE BUCK: Tony, should pitchers with a similar style and similar stuff be separated in your rotation to increase their effectiveness and prevent the opposition of using one pitcher to gauge another within a certain series? And if so, is this truer in the playoffs than in the regular season?

TONY LA RUSSA: Absolutely. You want to try to create different looks for the other side. What you want to have is the luxury of having pitchers with varying or different styles, different stuff. Some times you get bogged down; I think bogged may be exaggerating a little bit, but you have a problem when your best

TEAM MANAGEMENT

pitchers have similar stuff. What you don't want to do is to take one of your best pitchers out of the rotation because he's a lot like some other guy who's in your rotation. However, I can remember the Baltimore clubs when I first came into the league, and they had those great rotations that had Cuellar throwing left-hand screw balls, Palmer throwing overhand fast balls, McNally throwing curve balls, and they would go with somebody like Wally Bunker throwing sinkers. That creates so many problems for the other side. It definitely is the best way to try to set up your rotation. It really has more importance during the season. The playoffs are such a fierce crapshoot; you send your best players out there and don't worry about complementing styles.

JOE BUCK: **Tony, when a team brings in a lot of new players during the off-season, how does it affect the strategy and personal coaching approach of a manager in the upcoming season?**

TONY LA RUSSA: That's a good question, because one of the most important parts of managing or coaching is getting to know your player. You really want to figure out where he's strong and where he's weak. Part of coaching or managing is to put your players in situations where they can be successful. By that, I mean utilize their strength and avoid those situations where they'll be unsuccessful. Play away from their weakness. Unless you really get to know your player, it's hard to do that. You like to have some continuity to your roster, because once you learn about a player, you feel like you'll have a better chance to have him be as good as he can be. With that said, if there's one thing true about major league baseball in the last several years, there's a tremendous turnover every year. So there's a real priority in trying to evaluate players in the league who are not on your club. We spend a lot of time evaluating players who play against us just because you may have them the next year, and you're not starting from scratch. So, I think my answer is: it does affect you because you want to learn about them as soon as you can, but you ought to try to learn whenever you get a chance to see them, not just wait until they get on your club.

TEAM MANAGEMENT

JOE BUCK: Tony, how do you determine when a young catcher is experienced enough to call his own game?

TONY LA RUSSA: By definition, he's not experienced enough to call his own game. But here's the problem: Unless you let him call his game, how is he ever going to be experienced? People make mistakes with not trusting a young catcher with the game, and he never grows. They'll try to call the entire game from the bench. That has a lot of problems. If you try to call the game from the bench, you're really not seeing all the little nuances a catcher sees behind the plate. The coach on the bench is not receiving the ball, so he's not seeing the stuff and how that changes. He's not seeing the different messages the hitter sends you when he's standing at the plate. What we try to do when we do have young catchers here with the Cardinals is try to prep them. Dave Duncan is a master, and he's done this very successfully over the years with young catchers. He spends a lot of time with them before the game, talking about our pitcher, who's going to pitch that day, and our relievers. He also goes very carefully over the lineup that they're going to face. So, the answer for us is to take a young catcher like an Eli Marrero and prep him. Give him as much information as you can. Send him out there. Give him his own responsibility, and always be there from the bench in case he needs some help.

JOE BUCK: Tony, when you put together your ideal twenty-five-man roster, how many players do you want at each position?

TONY LA RUSSA: Half of your roster, or a little less than half of your roster, is going to be pitchers. So what you want to do is to have the ideal situation, which would be four quality starters. You probably want to go with a 10 or 11 man pitching staff. Of the four starters, and the other seven pitchers on the staff, you probably want to have four or five that are real specialty types. That leaves you two or three guys who can really swing. It can be the fifth starter who jumps in there occasionally. It can be another reliever or two who can give you innings, depending on the game

TEAM MANAGEMENT

situation. When you look at your position players, you want to have a nucleus. You want to have your basic outfield, which is usually a three spot. You want to look at your basic infield. So that's three and four, that's seven. Seven and 11, that's 18. That leaves you seven guys you can use. You can have a couple of specialty spots, such as a great pinch-hitter or a great pinch-runner, and another three or four players who have great versatility. You want to have a classic fourth outfielder, but you definitely want to have the classic infielder and a couple or three guys who can play different positions.

JOE BUCK: **Tony, when picking the twenty-fifth guy on your active roster, do you favor keeping an extra pitcher or an extra hitter, and is it different in a DH league?**

TONY LA RUSSA: There is some difference between the American and the National League. If you were in the American League where you don't use the bench nearly as often during the course of the game, it's not nearly as important to have a deep position player on the bench as it would be to have that extra pitcher. In the American League, with the way runs are scored, very often that extra pitcher comes into play more often than the extra player does. Now, how about a National League club? A lot depends on the type of rotation you have. If you have a rotation that's established and will consistently get you into the last three innings of the game, then you would definitely prefer to have that extra player be a position player. You'll need that extra guy for the different switches and all the game situations that arise in the National League. More than anything else, if you don't have that type of depth in the rotation, pitching gets hurt faster than anything else. You have to protect your pitching before you protect a few moves that you might want to make in the game.

TEAM MANAGEMENT

JOE BUCK: Tony, two guys play the same position. One tends to coast on raw ability while the other has less talent but works hard and has a lot of heart. Which would you keep on your team?

TONY LA RUSSA: I think the answer the fans want to hear is probably the one that should be the answer. If a guy is playing to his max, and he plays with a lot of heart, that guy gives you a better chance to win. So not only will you rely on what he brings, you will know what he has, and he's going to have it there for you everyday. And there's a ruboff effect with his teammates. His teammates like a player who's going out there giving you his best shot, even if he's a little short. He's more inspirational, and for all of those reasons you would tend to put that guy on the roster. There's a negative effect when the teammates look at a player who has a lot of ability but is half-stepping, as we say. He's not going out there making the commitment to practice or to play hard. He's there today, gone tomorrow. You lose games with that kind of unreliability. However, here's one of the key calls. You really have to understand the talent. If a player does not have very good talent but a lot of heart, and another guy has great talent and is coasting some, that difference isn't good enough to keep him off the club.

JOE BUCK: Tony, is the pre-game batting and fielding practice routine fans see as they arrive at the ballpark designed to get the players loose, or are you working on particular problems with certain ball players?

TONY LA RUSSA: The answer is: All of the above. By that I mean, when you come to the park on a particular day you'll see some of all of that. There may be players just out there getting loose. In other words, if you feel good about your game, if you feel like you have good defensive timing, and if you feel good at the plate, then all batting practice and fielding practice should do is just get yourself loose. Get a little feel back into your bat and your glove and your arm. You don't want to push it too far. However, on the other case, if you're struggling, then the best recipe for having a

TEAM MANAGEMENT

problem is to work. What you would have done before you take the field is, you would have sat with the manager or the coach. You might have gone into the underground cage to get a few things done mechanically. You might have talked about defensively why you're struggling, why you're not throwing the ball well, or why you're fielding poorly. So practice that day for a guy who's struggling has much more of a specific point they want to accomplish, and you'll see much more intensity. It really depends on where the player is that day.

JOE BUCK: Tony, how much actual teaching or coaching of fundamentals actually goes on during the season?

TONY LA RUSSA: A lot more today than it used to be for a lot of reasons. Back in the days when there were stronger and more developed minor league systems — in the sense you had to really raise yourself through the minor league system before you got to the big leagues — you learned to play the game at a much different level than you do now. Nowadays, if you have talent, you're going to get to the big leagues quickly. With that, you lose some of this preparation and some of the nitty-gritty about how the game is supposed to be played. There's a much bigger priority nowadays at the big league level to continue teaching and coaching, as opposed to what it used to be. The other thing that happens is: Some of the very talented athletes kind of get by on their ability, and as they're coming up, coaches — whether it's high school, college, or even some times the minor leagues — they don't want to get on the wrong side of the talented athlete, so they don't push to coach them. What happens when they get to the big leagues is that they don't have that attitude or ethic about wanting to learn and wanting to improve, and that's why it's so important to teach. By the way, the Cardinals do a very good job. They're very insistent the game be played the Cardinal way, and that's really important. However, because of experience, there's still coaching that goes on at the big league level.

TEAM MANAGEMENT

JOE BUCK: Tony, it's September and you've expanded the roster by bringing up some minor leaguers. What are you looking at as you evaluate these young players?

TONY LA RUSSA: First thing you want to do in September is evaluate the chance you're giving them. You've got to be very careful with the September call-up. It's a different time of the year. If you've got a ball club in contention, you're not going to give them much playing time. If you have a ball club out of contention, it's not the same pressure. It can be one of those things where the player is just out there with not the same intensity against him as he would be from the heat of the season. So, you want to look at the type of year your club is having. You also want to look at what kind of chances you give him. If you gave him 10 at bats in the first week and 10 at bats at the end of September, that's really not enough to say he can hit or not hit. I think the classic situation would be: If you have a guy play every day in September, you give him 20 or 25 games, and he gets to 80 to 100 at bats, then you might have a very good indication whether this guy can play, can hit, or not. What you want to gauge more than anything else is whether this player is awed by the big leagues. You want to judge his talent, but some players feel very comfortable in the big leagues right away while others never get comfortable.

JOE BUCK: Tony, when an opposing pitcher is in a rhythm, so to speak, what can the offense do to try to break that rhythm?

TONY LA RUSSA: I think that's one of those situations you don't like to get into because that means he's generating a lot of outs, usually quickly, and your offense is stagnating. There are some gamesmanship things the clubs will try — stepping in and out of the box, disrupting his wind-up — that's something that can be done, and depending on how emotionally wound up the guy is, that can work for you. I think you really want to try to look at his pattern: How is he getting the outs? Is he getting the outs with a lot of strike ones? Then, maybe even though you're behind, you may want to be more aggressive and swing early, because some

TEAM MANAGEMENT

of these players, if you give them strike one, then they really start working the corners and the at bats get tougher and tougher. If a guy is having trouble throwing strikes, you may want to take a few pitches. Usually, what you want to do is to vary how the hitters swing early in the count versus making them take a few pitches. Last but not least, if you get any chance with a runner on base, you really want to push the running game or the hit-and-run, because that's one way to generate some momentum and maybe catch a base hit that breaks open an inning. Anything like that will disrupt a guy going very well.

JOE BUCK: Tony, other than sending the runners to the plate, what are the typical responsibilities of a third base coach?

TONY LA RUSSA: That's a great question, because I think it's one of those inside baseball things that, if you go to the ballpark and you watch closely, you can really add to your enjoyment. Watch different third base coaches. Just the first part — other than sending runners — that traffic cop responsibility is a crucial one. The game is won by stopping the other club from scoring and you scoring, so when you have a chance to score, anytime he's the traffic cop, that's very important. You watch where they position themselves and what they're watching for as keys as to whether they send runners. It's all very important. The other things I think make up a good third base coach include having a feel for the game — 100 percent concentration. I feel a good third base coach is like a manager in waiting, a guy who manages even though he doesn't have the responsibility to call the different plays. They handle the game like it's their ballgame. They know exactly what the score is, and they're looking around to know when to try to push, because maybe it's hard to score. You want to be more aggressive against the player who hardly ever gets a run-scoring situation against him, or if you have something good going and you want to back off. I think the most important key is for that guy to have great instincts and pay a lot of attention.

TEAM MANAGEMENT

JOE BUCK: Tony, what are the responsibilities of a first base coach?

TONY LA RUSSA: Here again, I think sometimes the first base coach is underemphasized. It may be a coach that you have on the staff for other reasons, maybe he has important teaching credentials, but when he goes out to first he just stands there. The very good first base coach is very helpful to the team's base running. Many times as the runner is running to first and rounding the base, he can give him a heads up and tell him to go for an extra base, because he sees a play right in front of him. He can be very helpful that way. Any of the situations that develop, he can yell at a runner to tag up if the ball's going deep to the outfield. He can remind the player, which is probably his biggest responsibility, this is where we are in this inning, this is the score, and your responsibility is to be very aggressive trying to break up a double play or go to first to third on a base hit. Or, because you're behind, he might remind you to be very careful and don't get doubled off on a line drive. When he's looking around, he'll remind you that the good throws are in left and center, but the poor throws are in right. In other words, you want to push it. The ball goes one way, so you want to be careful going the other way. The other thing they do is: They watch the pitcher's move, and they'll give the runners keys as to when to steal.

JOE BUCK: Tony, what qualities are most important in a pitching coach?

TONY LA RUSSA: When you talk about a rounded set of responsibilities, when you say what's most important, I think they're all important, because to be a successful pitcher, you need each of these areas covered. Some pitching coaches are better in some areas than in others, that's why you can see the best pitching coaches are good in everything. For example, mechanics are something everybody points to. Obviously, if you've got a pitcher with some mechanical problems, the pitching coach has to help him to improve his delivery, and that's one of his key responsibilities. Another one I think is very important is to

TEAM MANAGEMENT

understand a pitcher's style. A pitching coach should evaluate the kind of fast ball, breaking ball, off-speed pitch and make recommendations like, "Look, you don't have a 95-mile-per-hour fastball, you have a sinker, so this is how you should pitch according to your style." When you evaluate the style, you may say, "You really need to use your fastball in different ways, or you may need to add a different breaking ball, or your off-speed pitch is not good enough." So evaluating the style. I think the other two responsibilities he has are: One, give the pitcher an idea about hitters' strengths and weaknesses so he can attack them; and two, really be into the mental part of the pitcher's game, and more than anything be positive and help him with his confidence.

JOE BUCK: Tony, who determines when a player sits because of an injury — the player, the manager, or the trainer?

TONY LA RUSSA: It's a combination of the three. You've got to start with the player, obviously. It's his injury. You really want to encourage honesty, but he can't decide it all by himself. I say that because players will tend to be heroes. They'll look at the competition. They'll look at their responsibility to their team, to the organization, to the fans, and they'll go out there even when it would damage them if they did so. That's why what you want from a player is an honest assessment of how he feels: Is his arm sore? Is his hamstring sore? Back? Or whatever it is? Once he gives you the honest explanation of how he feels, then you want to have the trainer or the team doctor give a professional opinion. Either he needs rest, or it's just sore and you can push him out there. You give all that information to the manager, and he puts it together to see, "All right, I've been told this player is sore but can play and will not hurt himself anymore." You kind of figure maybe he's at 75 percent. The manager figures 75 percent of this player is better than a whole guy he would bring off the bench. Then the manager decides which way to go. Usually for me, I hate playing guys that are hurting. It gives the wrong message to the players on the bench who know they're ready to go.

TEAM MANAGEMENT

JOE BUCK: Tony, let's say you're in the playoffs with some very young players, a young ball club. What do you do to keep them from thinking about things and getting too nervous?

TONY LA RUSSA: One of the qualifiers right there, which gets you excited, is that you're in the playoffs, so there's no way that you get to the playoffs unless those very young players have already been exposed to the pressure and have already been successful. What you really want to talk to them about is when you played early in the season and when you played a game in September. A lot of those games that we won to get to the playoffs were really must-win, and you remember times when they were good and you talk to them about: How did you do that? How did you come through? You try to reinforce their confidence. What were they thinking? Things don't really change in the playoffs. It's just that the stakes are raised because now you're playing for a bigger prize. But the way you go about it is really the same. You want to try to focus on how you do your job. You know if you're a pitcher, an infielder, or an outfielder, you talk about offense, defense, whatever it is. A key thing with young players is to reinforce that they've had the season of experience, and they've learned in these situations. The other thing that you want to stress with a young player is to be aggressive, and when in doubt be aggressive. Nothing gets rid of nervousness better than to go out thinking, "I'm going to make something happen."

JOE BUCK: Tony, does playing on the artificial turf change anything about the way you manage or the way your ball club plays the game?

TONY LA RUSSA: Yes it does, I mean there are some differences. Obviously, as a hitter, you can think about it going into a ballgame. If you're going to hit the ball sharp on the ground four times, you believe you're going to get at least a hit, so it really encourages guys who try to hit the ball sharply on line or on the ground. Guys who elevate the ball are going to make more outs. I think speed and line-drive hitting is usually different in the whole park. It also

TEAM MANAGEMENT

affects the way you play the game and the type of personnel you might build your club around. The other thing is: Your outfield positioning. You want to protect the gaps, because when balls get through on turf, anybody who runs well is going to have three bases. It affects the bunting when you're talking about the little game, trying to sacrifice - especially in a National League park - trying to sacrifice players over on an artificial turf makes it tougher because the balls will get to the pitcher or the infielder quicker and truer. You may want to be more aggressive with how you handle the bunting game and start runners. There's no doubt it makes it quicker. It's a different game and not nearly as good a game as on grass.

JOE BUCK: Tony, during a game, who is responsible for the defensive positioning of the infield and outfield on your team?

TONY LA RUSSA: It starts with, as a series begins we get our coaches together, and we talk about their team and how we're going to play them. On our ball club, the guy that does so much work on this is Dave Duncan. You'll see him on the bench, and you'll see him making notes about where the ball goes. He takes about two hours after every game to transpose that on charts he keeps, for a lot of information, including where the ball goes. When we get ready to play whatever team, we'll pull the charts out. We'll also get the report from out advance scout, Joe Sparks, and he'll talk about what he's seen, how the player is swinging right now and what he would suggest. Dave looks at what he's got for information, and then we say, infield, outfield, this is where we play them. During the game, Jose Oquendo and Mark DeJohn will be involved with where the infielders will be positioned. Dave McKay looks at the positions for the outfield. Last but not least, the manager is supposed to pay attention to all of that, and during the game you can make an adjustment based on what you see as far as the game situation. You can see whether you're ahead or behind, who the hitter is, and who the pitcher is. So in the end, the manager can change the positioning.

TEAM MANAGEMENT

JOE BUCK: **Tony, who determines when it's time to lift the pitcher? Is it the pitching coach, the manager or both?**

TONY LA RUSSA: Here again, you may have some differences on certain clubs. Some managers will parcel out pieces of their responsibility. Just like on an earlier show, we talked about pitchouts. Some managers let other coaches handle the pitchouts. I was taught the manager's butt is on the line the most, and it's your decision, your responsibility in the end for all these decisions. So, with making pitching changes, the final call has to come from the manager. How does that decision get made? If you have a good relationship with your pitching coach, and I think it's fair to say Dave and I have a good relationship, we're talking all the time about what we're seeing. We know a pitcher, especially if he's been with us before or you get to know him over the course of the year, you get to see little idiosyncrasies that tell you he's still got something left or he's about out of gas. So during the game, Dave and I are communicating all the time. The one thing you do find is that Dave is very loyal to his pitchers and always wants the starters to go a little bit more, because he wants them to have a decision. The manager has to be more objective. In the end, where there's a disagreement, the manager, in this case with St. Louis, I make the call.

JOE BUCK: **Tony, how do you determine your starting pitching rotation, or more importantly, when do you determine your starting pitching rotation?**

TONY LA RUSSA: I'm not sure at what point you pick a perspective for this question. If you talk about it out of spring training, your starting rotation is picked from the five players that give you the best chance to win. You probably go to camp with an idea of how many of them there are — this year it was four of them, but usually you have an idea of at least three of them, and you start looking at the first month or six weeks of the season. You try to see, by putting each guy in one, two, and three, four or five, what's their best chance to get off to a great start, because if they

TEAM MANAGEMENT

win, your club wins. The better start they get, the better start our club gets. You pick the pitchers from the array of players, and what you're looking for in a starting pitcher is more than two pitches. If he has four, he's wonderful, but he has to have at least three, otherwise you can't get through the lineup. You look for some stamina, but that's something that can be trained. Then you look for a little difference in styles. You hate to put guys who are very close to each other next to each other in the rotation. Those are some of the factors you look at, and then you try to trot them out, hopefully, all year long.

JOE BUCK: Tony, how do you decide how many pitchers to carry on the roster?

TONY LA RUSSA: What a terrific question this is, because this is part of why evaluating your ball club is so important, and the number will differ. If I go back to years ago, and I'm talking about years and years ago, pitching staffs sometimes had eight, nine, or 10 pitchers, and the reason they did that was they had one or two things happening. The starting pitchers were coming out every four days, so four of the guys were starters and those starters were pitching seven, eight, or nine innings, so you only needed four or five, maybe six relievers. However, as you've gone to five starters, right away that's an extra pitcher on your staff. The most important thing you try to decide nowadays is how much you can expect from each and every starter. Right now, with the 2001 club, we think that Kile and Hermanson have a lot of stamina here early in the season, but we're worried about pushing Andy. We're worried about pushing Morris and Ankiel. One thing you don't want to do is: You don't want to be pitching short to where the relievers that you have leaving camp are used so often in the first month or two that they burn out. Over the long course of the season, if your relievers are not as good late in the season as they are early, you don't have any chance to win. So we've chosen 12 very early.

TEAM MANAGEMENT

JOE BUCK: **Tony, when a young player comes to the big leagues, what do you do to keep their confidence up while they try to learn at this level?**

TONY LA RUSSA: Mostly, it's a matter of using common sense. By that I mean keeping confidence up is directly related to being positive with them. That's also directly related to them doing good enough so you can be positive. If a player's going out there and striking out four times in the three games you play him, you've got to point out something he's doing wrong. And, usually, if you talk to a young player in negative terms, they start getting worried and depressed. In fact, it even happens with veterans. So what we try to do is stay positive with them. You also try to make a point that baseball is a game to be learned, and experience is a great equalizer. What you really want to do early in your career is: You want to learn to play the game right, whether it's offensive, defensive, pitching, or whatever. You try to maintain a positive tone to the teaching. However, you really don't want a young player to come in and think he has all the answers, and he's got everything figured out. It's talking in positive terms, it's trying to give the basic fundamentals, and it's also work. Young players need to work to refine these skills.

JOE BUCK: **Tony, what exactly is the role of bench coach, and how important is he to your team's success?**

TONY LA RUSSA: That is a very interesting question that's been true for years, and I think it really relates to the manager. A manager has to be very honest about what he feels comfortable with in the game. If you've got a pitcher who's a manager, for example, I think he would have a lot of confidence and that he would understand the defensive side, getting guys out, and what a pitcher should do in a certain situation. However, he may not be nearly as comfortable on the offensive side as to when to run, when to steal, when to bunt, to hit-and-run, when to play for a run, and when to play for a bigger inning. Vice versa, if you've got an infielder that's a manager, he may not feel as qualified on the

TEAM MANAGEMENT

defensive side, such as whether this pitcher is losing his stuff or what's the pitch in a right situation. The bench coach can really complement the manager in the areas that he's not strong in. What you'll find is that managers have different opinions. Some managers don't mind giving a piece of the game away to a bench coach, such as control the running game and, "You call the pitchouts; I'll stay out of it." I was taught that a manager is responsible for everything. You're the guy who gets fired, so you take charge and you ask the bench coach for his opinion from time to time.

JOE BUCK: Tony, if a player's in a hitting slump, how do you go about trying to get him back on track?

TONY LA RUSSA: There are several keys, and there are two on the opposite ends of the spectrum. Some guys fall in a slump because they're just mentally and physically fried. So sometimes a guy that's slumping, the best thing he can do is take some time off. Don't take batting practice for a day or two, try to refresh yourself and clear your mind. Other guys, if you see that they're physically and mentally still in good shape but they're doing something wrong, then work is always a good therapy. I don't care if it's defense, a hitting slump, or whatever. Pick a couple of keys that are golden — a couple golden fundamentals — take them out there and work on them. For example, one of the golden fundamentals on hitting is keep your eye on the ball. You can do a couple of drills, but what you're trying to make sure he does is see the ball and stay on it. See the ball and stay on it. Another thing that's been very popular lately, and I think it's an improvement, is the use of video in hitting. You know, it's been used in other sports for a lot of years. Baseball's been a little slow and has been using it more from the pitching side. Mike Easler uses a lot of video to make the point to the player so that he sees himself doing the things wrong that Mike's talking about. It's very helpful.

TEAM MANAGEMENT

JOE BUCK: What do you look for in building a bench so that the five or six players you have fill in all the various roles that you're going to need?

TONY LA RUSSA: It's one of the challenges every year, and it changes with the makeup of your club. For example, especially in the National League, you have to have a couple or three spots off your bench that are quality pinch-hitters. It is one of the toughest jobs in baseball, and everybody understands that. Some guys can do it, and some guys can't. So you look for some player, or two or three that are good taking one at bat every two or three days. Then you want to complement your roster; you want to look at your outfield. Do you have guys you need to platoon because they're not everyday guys? Then you may need to have, if you've got left-handed hitting outfielders, then you have to have a couple of right-handers so you don't get mismatched against a left-handed pitcher. If you have, like we do, outfielders that can play a lot, then you really just need one outfielder that can play when one of the guys is hurt or if you want to maybe take advantage of one percentage move someday. In the infield, you evaluate the same way. If you have guys who are a real nucleus and can play a lot, then you can use more guys who are specialty pinch-hitters. Or if you have guys who aren't going to play very much, then you have to have a different situation. If you have some guy like McGwire with injuries, you may have to protect at that position like we do.

JOE BUCK: Tony, do you deviate from your regular pitching rotation for anything other than injuries? Or is the rotation more flexible?

TONY LA RUSSA: I think a regular rotation kind of means that the guys go in order, they follow each other, and it's usually a good idea to maintain that rotation as best you can. I think some of the ways you would deviate would be if the schedule provides an off day, and you have one guy struggling and four guys pitching very well. You may want to bang the guy that's struggling, keep the other four guys in rotation, and work the other guy back in when

TEAM MANAGEMENT

it's his turn again. You can, with enough lead-time — and we do this some — try to set match-ups for the schedule. If you look in May, and you start messing with your rotation, you can see that, if you pitch Darryl Kile on this day and you bring him forward every five days, he's going to miss a club he usually kills. So you may try to deviate a little bit to not lose that match-up. Some of those things I think are important parts of a manager's responsibility. Try to put your players in the best position to succeed.

JOE BUCK: Tony, do teams actually reflect a manager's philosophy or does the manager generally have to fit his philosophy to the players that he has?

TONY LA RUSSA: Clearly, the manager's philosophy has to match the players you have on your roster. Common sense says, if you're a guy who really likes a lot of power and if you have a bunch of singles hitters, what are you going to do — have everybody swing for the fences? Or you're a guy that likes to run, and you don't have anybody who can run, are you going to run guys who can't run? No, I think part of the strategy of the ball club is, depending on the players you have, if you have a certain type of offense, that's the offense you play. If you have a certain type of pitching staff, that's the way you try to pitch. The word "philosophy," I think, has a different look to it besides strategy, and there is a way to play. There are some managers who are more aggressive, while some managers are more conservative. I think to the extent the players, coaching staff, and manager are on the same page, it's kind of neat to see the philosophy be the same. I don't care who gets the credit for where it started and who follows it, but what you want to try to do is: You have to remember this a competition. The philosophy of your team should be very competitive, very aggressive, and remember that you're not there to make money and generate stats. You're there to win games, and I think that philosophy's very healthy for everybody involved.

TEAM MANAGEMENT

JOE BUCK: Tony, are pre-game warm-ups a set routine for everybody, or do the players each choose what they're going to do each day?

TONY LA RUSSA: It's a combination of both. You're expected, and you need to do certain things as a position player to satisfy the staff and get ready for the game. For example, you need to do something defensive. You need to do something to get your body loose and warm. You need to get your arm loose. If you're an infielder, you need to take some ground balls. You need to work at throwing to second base and first base. If you're an outfielder, you need to work that day on the conditions. You've got to take balls off the bat to see if the ball is carrying and which way the wind is going. You need to take some ground balls or fungos and then make a few throws to get your arm loose. So those things are required. Then each player also has a lot of individual opportunity to refine his workout. Some guys, such as maybe Fernando Vina, have a certain routine they uses every day — like ground balls at him, left, right, and a lot of double plays. So, you give them some basics they have to do, and then the players will do more or less depending on how much they need. A catcher like Mike Matheny and Eli Marrero, you will see them play long toss every day because that's part of their routine. It's the same thing with hitting; there are certain basic things, and anything more the guy needs, we're always willing to give it to him.

JOE BUCK: Tony, do your first base and third base coaches have other duties throughout the season?

TONY LA RUSSA: Absolutely. Our coaches have a lot of stuff they do. For example, our first base coach, Dave McKay, he works with outfielders defensively. Everybody who watches Mark McGwire hit batting practice knows that Dave McKay throws batting practice to Mark's group. Dave is also involved with our base runners. Then, we have the pitcher's offense. Dave is one of our coaches who gets involved making sure the pitchers are doing fundamental things correctly in their practice, whether they're slug bunting,

TEAM MANAGEMENT

bunting, or taking their offensive swing. So Dave does a lot of other things besides being at first base, making sure they run the bases properly. Jose Oquendo is an outstanding infielder who gets very involved with our infield play. He'll work with any of our infielders before the game or talk to them after the game — talk to them during the game about different plays. He also has to throw batting practice. I think an important part of a third base coach's job is: He has to spend a lot of time analyzing the other side, especially the manager's or the third base coach's aggressiveness against them, and the type of arms the outfielders have so he can decide when to push and when to hold.

JOE BUCK: Tony, how does a manager handle the situation when a player runs through a hold sign at third base, and does it matter if he scores anyway?

TONY LA RUSSA: That's one of those things during the course of the season you don't get all that crazy about in terms of calling a player out in front of everybody, embarrassing him, and making a big issue of it. Usually it happens because the player is running full speed, and he's really hustling. The third base coach has a tough decision and gives him a late look, and the runner just may not be able to stop in time or feel, "Hey, I've already gone so far and I'm going to go ahead." I mean, it's usually not done with the intent, "Hey, I don't care who the third base coach is, I'm going to make my own decision." Usually, if he scores, you laugh about it. If he doesn't score, you say, "Man you see, you should have paid attention. That third base coach knows what he's doing." If you ever have a feeling a player is defying the authority of any of your coaches, whether it's the first base coach or the third base coach, and he's playing his own game, that's when you step in and say, "Now look, let's talk about this. The coaches coach, the manager manages, and the players play." Through all the years I've been around, I've never seen a player purposely try to show up a coach and disrespect him by running through a stop sign.

TEAM MANAGEMENT

JOE BUCK: Tony, do you plan ahead to give your bench players enough playing time to stay sharp? Or is this just one of the many things a manager has to keep in mind as the games go along?

TONY LA RUSSA: Here's another one of the great questions that come up with fans. Do you play a set lineup all the time, or do you mix and match? Not because of injuries, because everybody knows you have to do that, but because you want to do it. I think it comes down to philosophy and what you were taught. What I was taught, and I obviously believe in it because that's the way I do it, is: If you have a core of players, that core of players should play the great majority of the games. The majority of the games could be four or five games in a week, six games in a week, but not all seven, and that helps that guy stay fresh because we're going to play for six months. You want your players who are key to have something left when you get to August, September and, hopefully, October. At the same time, your bench players have to play enough, not just a pinch-hit once in a while or a double-switch at bat. They have to play enough to where their game is alive, because those same bench guys will come up late in the game they're not starting, and if they get a base hit, then you win and, if they're out of timing, then you lose. It makes a lot of sense to give them enough time to stay sharp. It keeps your regulars fresh, and then you push your nucleus toward the end of the season.

JOE BUCK: Tony, how much does a manager coach his coaches? Is training them part of your job?

TONY LA RUSSA: That's an interesting question. I believe that's the first time I've ever been asked that. Unfortunately, in my situation the coaches coach the manager. When we get around to pitching, Dave Duncan is coaching Tony about pitching. I can remember when I first started managing, Charlie Lau coached me about hitting. In fact, and this is a good memory for me, when I first started managing, Jim Leyland was my first base coach. He had managed 13 years in the minor leagues, and I'd managed two. So

TEAM MANAGEMENT

Jim would coach me on managing. I think, in a lot of situations, what a manager should do for his coaches is to have them understand the style of play he thinks fits the ball club and gives the best chance to win. So you tell your outfield coach, "Hey, our outfielders need to do A, B, C." I think it's very important for the coach to know what the manager expects, so he can translate that to his outfield. It's the same thing with the infield and the same thing with the hitting coach. I think you want to tell your hitting coach, "Look, with the personnel and for good baseball, this is the type of offense we need to have." We need to have some players who can handle a bat. They need to know what to do in an RBI situation, how to work the count, and draw a base on balls. I think all of that comes from communicating with your coaches.

LINEUPS

JOE BUCK: Tony, say you have a player who is 2 for 24 lifetime against a certain pitcher, but he hits fine against other guys with similar stuff. Do you figure it's just a fluke or do you start someone else?

TONY LA RUSSA: I think 2 for 24 is enough career history where you start to think, "Man, this is not a good match-up." You see that occur and why is that? The game is so mental; maybe you had some tough days against the guy. In the back of your mind, even though you're trying to be positive, you think, "Man, this guy's got my number. I just can't see the ball." I remember a notable example back in Chicago: Carlton Fisk, who hit everybody, had a tough time against Jack Morris. Finally I asked him — I think he was 3 for 35. It was just because of his delivery; he couldn't pick up the pitch. If you can't see the ball or you think you have some type of problem, you're just asking for trouble and you're trying to bury your hitter. What you would do is: 2 for 24 would be a real strong indicator that if you need to rest a player, this would be a great time to rest him. If it turns out that in a particular series a player is red hot and you don't want to take him out, then maybe there'll be a situation during the course of the season or two or three seasons where you may let him face the pitcher once in a while. If he gets it going and if he hits against him, then he's fine. If not, I wouldn't risk it. But 2 for 24 is a red light that says, "Sit him down."

JOE BUCK: Okay, Tony La Russa, here's today's question. One of your regulars is swinging a hot bat, but he doesn't have a hit in 25 at bats against the opposing team's starter. Do you give him that day off?

TONY LA RUSSA: I would say, generally, that's the kind of statistic that gets your attention. I think most of the time statistics can be abused, but there is a use for them, and over the course of a long season most players takes a break here or there. They need a day off mentally as well as physically. You would look at success like that, where for some reason — maybe he doesn't pick the ball up

LINEUPS

off the pitcher, his release point may be very difficult for him to see — that would be the day that you would sit him, even if he were real hot. What usually happens with just that one day's break, you save him that very tough match-up so when he goes back out there the next day, he'll still be confident and you won't have him hitting in a situation where he's not likely to succeed. In fact, that's what managing is: You try to put guys to their strengths and avoid areas or situations that are not good for them.

JOE BUCK: Tony, how do you decide when to sit a slumping hitter?

TONY LA RUSSA: That's a tough call. I think you try to read: Where did the slump come from? Sometimes it comes from fatigue, and then the obvious answer is to just rest the player, let him get off his feet, watch a couple games, get his strength back, and all of a sudden his bat will get quick and his confidence will go up. Sometimes a slump comes because a player is a little injured and starts favoring his leg or his wrist, something like that. Same answer as before: You want to rest the guy. Very often something mental happens to a hitter. He goes a couple of days without a base hit — maybe he hit the ball fine, but he didn't get hits — and he starts pressing. When you see that, the slump is more mental than anything else is and you can do a couple things. One, you can rest him. Another, you can switch him in the batting order. Sometimes just giving him a different responsibility will give the hitter a fresh look. There's always one point you can go to — no matter if it's a slumping hitter or slumping fielder — work is great therapy. You can bring a guy out for extra work. Usually, when a hitter's having trouble getting base hits, you've got to simplify and go back to fundamentals to just see the ball and try to put the ball in play. A lot of times you just hit the ball back to the middle. So either you work, rest, or change him in the lineup as the keys to ending a slump.

LINEUPS

JOE BUCK: **Tony, rarely are there nine perfectly suited hitters in a batting lineup. So, when you put a lineup together, where do you start?**

TONY LA RUSSA: That's a great question. I think you have to look at the assets on your club. You look at your most dangerous hitter and you go from there. You want that player to hit in a spot where he can be the most productive for your team to score runs. Then you go to your next most productive. If you have somebody ideally suited to a particular spot in the lineup, then you shouldn't move him. You can start from that. For example, Delino DeShields proved last year that he's an excellent top of the lineup, leadoff type guy. Well, even though Delino may be red hot at the time, you really don't start thinking about him in some other place. I think it's the guys suited to certain spots that help you get your lineup started more than anything. There's the most dangerous guy; you want to put him where you think he can do the most damage, and then you want to start building the protection around him. I think you also want to consider when you make out a lineup: Who's the other pitcher and who's in their bullpen? If you have a guy who's a real tough starter, you may want to put your toughest lineup in the order because you know you're going to face him deep in the game. If they have a very tough bullpen, you may want to set the lineup so you can compete against their bullpen.

JOE BUCK: **Okay Tony, here's today's question. How do you go about putting your players into a batting order?**

TONY LA RUSSA: You look at the classic pieces of the formula that have been passed along from baseball managers and coaches for years. For the top of the lineup, you want on-base percentage guys, and in the middle of the lineup, the third spot is probably your most complete hitter. He's the player who's got the best chance to hit for an average, run enough to stay out of a double play, and also has some extra-base pop. Your fourth and fifth spots are your more power players, the ones who have the knack of producing a base hit with runners in scoring position.

LINEUPS

Sixth spot is still a very good RBI spot, but not quite as tough as fourth or fifth. As you get down to the bottom, one thing that I like to do is to try to stretch the lineup. You don't want to just jam pack all your hitters in the first four or five spots; pretty soon you find out that you are not playing but six innings of baseball instead of nine. So you like to try to have some legitimate hitters in your seventh and eighth spot in the National League. I think there are two other important issues. As often as you can, try to have an eighth place hitter that's a legitimate offensive player, especially with some speed. And I think the leadoff hitter should be a guy who can drive in a run as often as he can.

JOE BUCK: Tony, here is today's question. You have a player who gets on base a lot but is slow and can't run. Do you bat him at the top of the order because of his on-base percentage or do you drop him down because of his lack of speed?

TONY LA RUSSA: It really depends on what your options are and how slow he actually is. If you are searching for a top-of-the-lineup guy who can set the table for your RBI types in the middle, and if you don't have anyone like that who has very good speed, then the fact that you have a slow runner who can get on base a lot may give you more scoring opportunities than some other guy who runs very well but is never on base. You have to look at your alternatives. Although, if he is very slow and is a clogger, then you have to be very careful because you don't want him in front of your other base runners who are running well. He is going to be a one-base-at-a-time player where your other players can go two bases and he is always stopping them from doing it. I have seen one guy, Brian Downing, who used to hit leadoff. He used to have a high on-base percentage, hit for extra bases, did not have real good speed but wasn't deadly slow. He just wasn't a good runner, but he made an effective leadoff man. You may want to use the on-base percentage guy up at the top because that's the number one criteria for the top of your lineup.

LINEUPS

JOE BUCK: Which is more important to a leadoff hitter - on-base percentage or the ability to steal bases? And is there a minimum on-base percentage a player must maintain to hit leadoff?

TONY LA RUSSA: I would rather not have to make that decision or have to make that judgment. In other words, what you like to have is the leadoff hitter who gets on base and then can turn that one base, whether it's a walk or a single, into more with a stolen base of second or third. If you had to choose between the two, I think it's more important to get on base. On-base percentage is very important, unless you are a base clogger and you only go base-to-base, then you have to be very careful. Mark McGwire, for example, has an on-base percentage about .450 and walks a hundred-plus times. You hit McGwire first — and I am not talking about the argument about using up his power — I am talking about the fact that getting him on first base will clog all the bases. The ability to steal bases creates something from being able to get on base. It's very important for a leadoff man. As far as what your minimum percentage is, that would be attractive but it really depends on your ball club and what the alternatives are. If you don't have a lot of choices, somebody is going to have to hit up there and you would go for somebody that has some explosive speed. If you have a lot of choices, then you start to balance on-base percentage versus the ability to steal bases.

JOE BUCK: Tony, in selecting someone to bat second in your lineup, some managers look for a bat-control type guy who can bunt, move the runner over, what have you. How do you describe the classic number two hitter?

TONY LA RUSSA: I think the classic number two hitter depends on your leadoff hitter and your number three hitter. If you have a real speed, stolen base threat leading off, then it's very important that the number two guy do something to handle the count — take some pitches so the guy can steal the base, turn a single or a walk into a double. If you don't have that kind of player, then it's not

LINEUPS

nearly as important if you're a number two guy to be able to handle the bat and work the count. The other thing is: What about your third hitter? If you have a third hitter that's very dangerous, that two hitter can really take advantage of the fear the other side has, and he should be a threat that has some extra-base potential. Because the other side, if they know he's just a little ping, slap-type hitter, they'll just throw the ball down the middle, and if they give up a single there is no big cost. You want to work those guys into a bind, so they're worried about throwing a strike to a guy that's got extra-base pop, because they don't want the guy behind him to hit with someone extra on base. I think there are a lot of factors to consider. The classic number two hitter is very tough to find.

JOE BUCK: Okay Tony La Russa, here's today's question. What qualities do you look for in a number three hitter and how do they compare to the qualities you look for in a number five hitter?

TONY LA RUSSA: I think the number three hitter is probably going to be a little quicker as far as foot speed. Traditionally, number three is the most complete hitter on your ball club. By that I mean he's a guy who should be able to start a rally, finish a rally, and continue a rally, so that's why you look for foot speed. If you have a guy who is very slow and likely to hit into a double play, you may never get the cleanup hitter up that inning. So, one difference you see very often is that your five hitter may be a little slower and may be a little stronger. You may have more of a power-type guy in the five hole. Three is somebody you would think is a very complete hitter and gives you a plus in as many offensive categories as you can come up with.

JOE BUCK: Okay Tony La Russa, here's today's question. Cleanup hitters are paid to hit home runs and to drive in runs. To you, which one of these is more important?

TONY LA RUSSA: That's an easy one to answer. The game is really built around stopping the other club from scoring and you

LINEUPS

scoring runs, so I've seen very good cleanup hitters who hit 10 home runs and drive in 110 runs. The most important stat by far is how many runs you do drive in, and I think that's another important point about the fourth spot. There is an aura to being the fourth-place hitter, and I've seen a lot of good hitters that can hit third, fifth, and sixth, but as soon as you put them in the fourth spot, they really can't handle that cleanup pressure. They try to do more than they can, and they try to hit for more power. The very good cleanup hitter has a strong confidence factor, and he doesn't mind that extra pressure of being the big producer. Here is an example: You have runners on second and third — a lousy single is two runs. I would rather have a cleanup hitter who hits for a high average and who can get that base hit over the course of the year than a guy who hits .220 and maybe hits 30 home runs, because that's only 30 base hits.

JOE BUCK: **Tony, when putting together a batting order, what are you looking for in the five, six and seven slots?**

TONY LA RUSSA: Starting with fifth, that's a very critical spot because he's hitting behind the fourth guy. I think for most clubs, the fourth guy is a classic run producer. Most teams have the opinion that, as they go into a series, they can eliminate one of the guys on the other team's lineup, and if you don't have protection for your cleanup hitter with a good quality fifth hitter, you can take him right out of the game. So in the fifth spot, you're looking for a guy that's also a tough run producer. He could be the slowest guy on your club, but it makes no difference. The most important quality for the fifth-place hitter is the ability to hit with men on base and get a base hit that drives in runs. Power is nice, but the ability to get a hit with men on base is the most important. Sixth is like fifth, except it's one spot down and maybe not quite as dangerous. In the seventh spot, I think you have to be careful or you may have to use that seventh spot for a guy who's not a tough out, because you want to save the eighth spot in front of your pitcher. It helps — and this is one way to track how good a club is — if the seventh place hitter is a tough out. You can look at the '96 club, and Tom

LINEUPS

Pagnozzi hit seventh all year long for us. Look at how many big hits he got. If your seventh-place hitter is a good hitter, then you've got a good lineup and a very good club.

JOE BUCK: Tony, in the National League where the pitchers bat, what do you look for in a guy who hits eighth?

TONY LA RUSSA: I told our club when I first got here in '96, that I only had a couple of opinions about trying to manage in the National League from watching games on TV over the years. One was that pitchers should put a lot of attention into their offense, because if they get a base hit or a bunt, it almost always helps you score a run and can be very important. The other opinion was on the eighth spot. I never could understand why you would have an eighth place hitter who doesn't run well and is not a good offensive player, because if that eighth place hitter gets on, very often you use the pitcher to advance him into a scoring position. If the guy does not get on base because he's a bad hitter, all of a sudden you've got him making an out, then you've got the pitcher likely to make an out. You're giving up a couple innings a game or at least two innings a game. I don't think you're good enough to give up that edge. The other issue is: He may be a good hitter, but not a good runner. Try bunting over a slow runner from first to second with a pitcher against a tough bunt defense where the third baseman, first baseman, and pitcher are all crashing. This is very difficult to do and very tough to sacrifice. If you want to do something more aggressive. like starting the runner and play hit-and-run you can't do it if he doesn't run well. So my eighth place hitter is selected on the basis of on-base percentage and good legs.

LINEUPS

JOE BUCK: Tony, during the 1998 season you hit the pitcher eighth in your batting order. Why did you do it? And was it a one-time thing in 1998 or is it something we'll see periodically throughout the next few years?

TONY LA RUSSA: The answer to why did I do it is a little bit of how I was trained as a manager. I came from an organization with some people like Paul Richards and Bill Veeck that really challenged you to think about different strategies for different situations and not to get bogged down with the book. The book has a lot of good sense, but once in a while, something else makes better sense. If you look at our club last year, and in many cases this year, we don't have our number-two hitter who's a normal, hit the ball to the opposite field, get deep in the count — a classic Ted Sizemore, who did such a great job for the Cardinals. Our last year, we had either Brian (Jordan) or Ray (Lankford) hit second. Ray or Mark (McGwire) hit third, and Brian or Ray hit fourth. So our RBI guy is hitting second, third, and fourth. It makes sense to me, if the ninth place hitter is a position player, not the pitcher, he's got a better chance to get on base for our RBI guys. The other thing it does, since Mark McGwire is hitting third, is as soon as you turn the lineup around he becomes a cleanup hitter, which is what a lot of people think would be better for us anyway. Will we do it this year? I think that whenever it makes sense, I wouldn't hesitate to get into it.

JOE BUCK: Tony, in the American League with the DH, is the guy who bats ninth automatically the worst hitter, or do you look for more of a second leadoff man?

TONY LA RUSSA: I think without question most clubs look at ninth as a second leadoff spot. It's just really common sense. As soon as a lineup turns over, you've got your leadoff, two, three, four — so if the ninth guy can be an on-base percentage guy, a second leadoff guy, then he will start rallies and make you a lot of runs. Very often I've had guys in the American League hit .300 batting ninth, and you'd have to explain to them how important

LINEUPS

they are to the offense. It's completely opposite as to hitting your worst guy ninth. I think that would tend to cut your runs scored rather than help them. So I think a lot of times the ninth-place guy is a good hitter, especially if he has good speed and on-base percentage. These are the things you look for in a number one and number two hitter. You want to set the table for three, four and five. Your number one statistic is on-base percentage. In the American League, the ninth spot is like the one and two spots. If you can get on base for the middle of your lineup, you're going to score a lot of runs. I don't think there's any doubt that, maybe some would question that, but almost everyone likes that ninth place hitter to be a tough out.

JOE BUCK: **When all eight regular position players are healthy, is it generally best to stick with the same batting order each game or juggle the lineup card occasionally?**

TONY LA RUSSA: Here's one of those questions that I think is the second guesser's delight when you lose a ball game and something's not working. If you stay with the same lineup, somebody's going to say, "Boy, make some changes, switch it around." If you switch it around and you get beat, then you're told you should just run the same guys out in the same spot all the time. Now, this doesn't address how much you use your bench. That would be another question. This one is, if you had the same eight guys, do you like to leave them alone in the same spots or do you like to juggle it? My preference is to try to form a nucleus of a lineup. You want the key guys in your lineup to feel comfortable and to come into a ballpark knowing what their assignment is going to be. So as much as you possibly can with the nucleus of the lineup, you probably want to have the same guys hit towards the front and towards the middle. However, in a particular series, you may face a very tough match-up where the guy that hits fifth is 0 for 20 against a pitcher that's facing you, and the guy that you hit seventh is 15 for 20. You may want to juggle to take advantage of some favorable match-ups. I think you want to be very careful when you juggle, but in any case you are always going with your best shot to win.

LINEUPS

JOE BUCK: Now Tony La Russa, here's today's baseball question. Is it important to you to have one or more switch-hitters in your lineup?

TONY LA RUSSA: I think it's important to have good hitters in your lineup. You look every year at the teams who are very successful, and these are the teams with good hitters. I've seen teams win a hundred games and be champions, and have all right-hand hitters. Generally, you won't find too many teams that have a lot of left-hand hitters and win a lot of games, because I think there is a trend or a fact in baseball showing that left-hand hitters can be neutralized by left-hand pitchers. The exception to this is the very best of the left-hand hitters, so what you look for is the best hitters. Here again, with all that said, there is no doubt that a switch-hitter is like, "Bonanza!" It's one of my favorite things to have switch-hitters, whether they are in the lineup or on the bench, because a switch-hitter makes it very difficult for the manager on the other side to make pitching changes. It makes it very difficult for him to set up how he's going to manage his bullpen because he knows when he makes a change, your hitter can just turn around. It's really important to have switch-hitters in your lineup, and it's also very important, probably more important actually, to have switch-hitters on your bench. That really defeats the way the other manager wants to use his bullpen.

JOE BUCK: During the game, how do you keep track of the other team's substitutions and who they still have left on their bench?

TONY LA RUSSA: There are two or three main ways. You can look at the big lineup card on the wall, and that is something that's kept up to date, whether you do it yourself or your bench coach commonly will do the scratching out whenever a replacement is made. You also have the smaller lineup cards that are exchanged between the umpires and the two clubs before the game starts. That's the one you keep in your hand. On that lineup card, you have the lineup listed and they also have to list all the players

LINEUPS

eligible to play. If you are away from the big card, you just look in your hand at the little card and figure out what goes on. This is also an area where a bench coach can be helpful if he's really paying attention and he's got a feel for what you're thinking about. For example, you may be looking at how you are going to use your pinch-hitters and he knows you're thinking about your side of the game. He can remind you they only have this player or that player available in their bullpen. These are all ways you keep track of it. The lineup cards and a bench coach both can be very helpful.

JOE BUCK: Tony, with a true power hitter in the lineup, how does he affect the guy hitting in front of him and what does the player batting behind him need to do to help protect him?

TONY LA RUSSA: This sounds a lot like a Mark McGwire question. The key part to add to this, though, is it's not just a true power hitter but it's a true power hitter who's a very good hitter. If you have good power but you can be pitched to easily, you don't pick up nearly the plusses that a hitter like Mark brings to our lineup. When you're also a very good hitter, the other side really fears you because they know that you're going to hit the ball solidly many times. If you have power, your solid hits are going to be for extra bases, and in fact, they can leave the park. So what does that do for you? The guy in front of you will really pick up a lot of extra pitches in the strike zone to hit. As soon as they throw you a pitch or two, they're going to look over the shoulder and see the big power hitter who's a good hitter waiting on deck. They'll say, "Look, I don't want to walk this guy and give this next hitter another run to drive in besides himself." The player hitting in front is in a great spot to hit. The player hitting behind has tremendous pressure and responsibility because the other side is not going to want to give in to that great power hitter that's a good hitter, and they will tend to want to pitch to the next guy. If the next guy has his own danger, like a Ray Lankford does, then you have the best of all worlds.

LINEUPS

JOE BUCK: Tony, how does a team compensate if you want to play one of those good field, no hit guys in the middle infield?

TONY LA RUSSA: One way you're compensating is you're always going to be in the game if you've got good pitching, because there's no substitute for that no matter how much offense a middle guy will provide. If he can't play effective defense at second, short, center, and catcher, he can't do enough offensively to overcome bad defense. So you want to be able to get the good pitching, the outs they generate, with the pitches they make and if you have somebody good offensively, that's even better. I mean, right now, there is just an amazing amount of shortstops and second basemen who are good offensively as well. However, if you had to pick between the two at an important defensive position, take the defensive player. How you compensate is: You want to have offense from other spots. The other factor is: There are ways for even that no-hit guy to be able to generate some offense. You may want him to really think about hitting the ball, if he's right-handed, from left-center over to right field. In other words, use the whole field. He shouldn't be one of these guys who swing from his butt and pops the ball up. You want him to be able to handle the bat with a hit-and-run or a bunt, so at least he could advance runners in some situations. However, I would never sacrifice offense for defense in that key of a spot.

JOE BUCK: Tony, some players are pretty vocal about liking to hit in a certain spot in the batting order and not liking to hit in other spots. Does it really make a difference where they hit? And if you've got one of those guys, do you typically let him have his way?

TONY LA RUSSA: It's a really hot topic here in St. Louis just because of what Mark McGwire has done in the three hole; so many people look at him as the classic cleanup guy, so he should be in the fourth spot. I think some perceive that Mark likes and wants to hit third. Mark has said many times that he will hit wherever the manager wants to place him. He just wants to help

LINEUPS

us win games. I think the key is that baseball is so mental, if you have a strong preference then you try to pay attention to that as a manager, looking at if it works and if it's what you think is best for your ball club. You pay attention to the hitters who like to hit at the top of the lineup, like to hit at the bottom, or don't like to hit at the bottom of the lineup or vice versa, or pitchers that prefer this situation or that. However, you can't let their wishes determine how you run your lineup or how you run your game. It comes down to how it mixes the best with the rest of the team. There are many times when you have players unhappy with their position in the lineup or their position on a pitching staff because you think they'd fit better in that situation. You try to weigh it all and come out with your best chance to win.

JOE BUCK: Tony, there's been a lot of talk about who to bat third, fourth, or fifth in your lineup. What are you looking to accomplish when you're making those lineup decisions?

TONY LA RUSSA: You're looking for your best chance to win, which is to complement the three hitters. For example, if there are two lefts and a right, you want to stick the right in between the lefts. If there are two rights and a left, it's not nearly as important, because right-handers face right-handers so often. I think with the classic lineup, the third place hitter is your best hitter and is the guy who gets on base the most, does the most damage, and can also run. If you look at the Cardinals with Mark hitting in the third spot, the only thing that he doesn't do there is run. What you also want from your fourth-place hitter is for him to be the guy who is the most productive driving in runs. So Mark definitely fits in that category. However, in our case, with Mark, you need to have somebody to protect him, and Ray Lankford was great that way. We're having this discussion this year, in the year 2000, because we've deepened our pool of who can hit in the middle of the lineup with a Jim Edmonds, Fernando Tatis now in his second year, and hopefully a healthy Eric Davis. So, three, four, five — three is the complete player, and four and five are guys that do well when they have runners in scoring position.

LINEUPS

JOE BUCK: **Tony, is there much that differentiates between a number six and a number seven hitter in your lineup?**

TONY LA RUSSA: Not really, the only difference is that one guy hits in front of the other. I think the thing you look at to make a difference is: Who hits fifth? For the simple fact that, if you play against a bullpen that has strong relief from the left side or the right side, you probably don't want to back up your hitters and make it easy for the other side to relieve against you, if you had a choice. If both your sixth and seventh spots are right hand hitters, it's not a key call. The fact is, a lot of baseball people think that seventh place, over the course of a season, gets as many RBI chances as sixth. I'm not sure I agree with that. I think sixth and seventh are really wonderful spots for a guy to not be quite as pressurized in his at bats and have many opportunities to get a lot of key hits. I do believe there is a difference in the National League, because as soon as you get to the last third of the lineup, your seventh-place hitter is followed by eighth and ninth. There's a difference in the last third of your lineup from the middle four, five and six spots, so I might look for somebody who had a little more speed to hit in the seventh spot, but it's not a key difference. I think the key thing is to complement the other players around him.

JOE BUCK: **Tony, if your starter was rocked the last time he pitched against a certain ball club, would you consider changing the rotation and using a different pitcher the next time you play that team?**

TONY LA RUSSA: It's something that you do consider. Normally you dismiss it, because hopefully there are reasons you can address why he did not pitch well against that club and give him a better chance the next time he plays against them. If you're looking at a guy who got rocked and there are things you can't solve, then you're going to be in trouble and there's no way that you're going to be able to protect him very long against other clubs. He's going to be vulnerable against everyone you play against. Once in a while you do face a club that a pitcher just

LINEUPS

seems to have the whammy when he pitches against them, and that's how you set up your rotation. Looking ahead, maybe you try to structure it where he doesn't pitch against them, and he misses it because of the way you set up the rotation. However, if it's just because he got beat up the last time he faced them and now it's a week later and he's facing them again, normally you have to stay with it. You just have to look at why he was hit so hard, so you do something different. There usually are things you can do different, such as you can make different pitches or he can just have a different style of pitching against them.

JOE BUCK: Tony, how does having a slugger like Mark McGwire impact the players hitting in front of him and behind him in the order and does it change the type of player you hit in those spots?

TONY LA RUSSA: This is a great question because we have a dramatic example with Mark McGwire, but there are other really tough and dangerous hitters in Major League Baseball. Other clubs have a similar type advantage, and it makes your lineup so much more dangerous to the club trying to beat you when the big slugger's playing. Why? His presence in the lineup means you need to get the hitters in front of him out, because you don't want him coming to bat with damage on base. Then, due to the fact he's in the lineup, all of the other hitters seem to relax a little more because the other team is not paying as much attention to them. The other team can't concentrate as much on them, so they'll take advantage of that lack of attention to get more pitches to hit, better pitches to hit, and do more damage. The guys behind him will find that, with the slugger on base, they'll have more opportunity to be productive. Who hits in front and behind him? To me, in front, the key thing is have a good strike zone to take advantage of the big guy being so dangerous, because if you get the count right they will have to challenge you and you can hurt them. The hitter behind him has to be somebody that's respected enough to force them to pitch to the slugger.

GAME DECISIONS

JOE BUCK: Tony, here is today's question. It is late in the game, two men on base, and the tying run at bat is a power hitter on a hot streak. Do you walk him or pitch to him and take your chances? In other words, do you put the tying run on?

TONY LA RUSSA: I think that sometimes you put the winning run on. It's the same type of factors. Usually, it has to be late in the game when you're really counting outs, so it really needs to be the eighth or the ninth. If you do it earlier, it may just break the game open. If it's the eighth or the ninth, and the hitter is really hot, you would consider it. The key really is: Who is the on deck player. If you think you have a real advantage against him, and he is not nearly as tough an out in this situation, then it's a good play. In many of those situations, you decide who can hurt you the worst. You don't want to walk into the clubhouse having the player most likely to beat you be the one who beats you. So, you would walk a tying run to get to the player that you have the better shot against. I have even used that — it's against the baseball book — but occasionally you put the winning run on base if you have the advantage against the next batter.

JOE BUCK: Okay Tony, here is today's question. Your team has an early threat going, first and second nobody out. How do you decide whether to be conservative that inning or play for the big inning?

TONY LA RUSSA: You put several factors together. It is really one of the great calls, and, in fact, you love to have it. Anytime you have first and second with nobody out, you have a real chance to score. I think some of the factors that you put together with your hitter at bat is: Who is this guy and how likely is he to do something that will keep the inning going and maybe make it a big inning? If it's one of your big productive hitters, then you don't want to take the bat out of his hands with a bunt. If it is a player who is not really one of your top tough outs, if he does something like lay a bunt down and advance runners then he has done something productive offensively. You always want to check the

GAME DECISIONS

inning and the score. It may be later in the game where every run you get is gold, because it means the other club has got to get two. So you may, with a good hitter, be more likely to give up the out to take a better chance at a run. Last, but not least, you look at the kind of a game that is being played. Maybe you have an outstanding guy pitching against you, and runs are at a premium. If you get first and second with nobody out, you'd better try to get at least one run there because you may not have very many opportunities left in that game.

JOE BUCK: Okay, Tony, here is today's question. It's a crucial game late in a pennant race. Your ace pitcher has only three days' rest. Do you start him anyway, or go with your fourth starter who has been just average all season?

TONY LA RUSSA: I definitely think the answer is: You would go with your ace pitcher with three days' rest, especially if you were able to do what we try to do all year long — working guys with four days' rest and being careful with them. What you would hope you have is a fresh enough pitcher whom you could use that one day short of rest on an infrequent basis when you really need it the most. We have done that in the past. You take care of your pitching staff and your players so you can push them in the last two months of the season, when the games are really counting down. No doubt in my mind: If the pitcher has not been abused, the ace would go with three days' rest and the fourth guy would just go in the bullpen.

JOE BUCK: Okay, Tony, here's today's question. If you pull the infield in, you may get a runner at home but you also increase the batter's chances for getting one through the infield. When do you decide to pull the infield in?

TONY LA RUSSA: If you think about it, the key call has to be: How much does that potential run really hurt you if he scores? That really is what determines your decision. If that run at third should

GAME DECISIONS

score, and really hurt your chances to win, then you've got to do whatever you can to shut it off, even if it opens up the risk for a bigger inning. I've even seen it done by other clubs - plus I've done it - when it's second and third and one out, where a base hit is not just one but it's two; that can really blow your chances. However, the key thing is: If you can live allowing that run to score, you play the infield back. The other factor is: Who's the runner at third, and who's the hitter? For example, if a Kenny Lofton is the hitter and he happens to get on first, and if it's because you brought the infield in, he's likely to steal second and third. Then it really is going to be two runs, not one, so you may just decide to give up that run. It's really a tough call. I think the answer is: If you can afford to, let that run on third score. If you can't, then you've got to try to cut it off.

JOE BUCK: Tony, here is today's question. It is the top of the eighth inning and your team is ahead by one run. Your strong hitting/weak fielding infielder has just batted in the seventh inning. Do you replace him now with a better fielder or do you wait until the ninth inning to make that defensive replacement?

TONY LA RUSSA: That is a tough call for several reasons. Obviously, it makes sense, if he has just hit, to put your better defense in there for the next six outs. But the other problem you try to figure out is: How likely is it you can keep the score where it is? What will happen is if the other team comes back to tie or you get behind, that better hitting infielder would have hit in the ninth, and now he's out of the game. So you have got to be very careful with that. Normally, if you have a ball club where you have to have defensive replacements for good hitters, it's a tough way to go. The defensive player is always under the gun. The offensive player, unless he really knows he's a defensive liability, usually has a loss of confidence. He thinks that he's not as good a player, or he doesn't hit as well. The idea is to try to improve the defensive player. I think if you put it as the question is asked - if you had the lead - you want to play your best defense. If the player is a good hitter and not a great fielder, you would take him out after he hits after seven.

GAME DECISIONS

JOE BUCK: In a key late-inning situation, one of your right-handed relievers is scheduled to face a right-handed hitter who has gotten six straight hits against him. The pitcher has retired all four batters he's faced. Do you leave him in?

TONY LA RUSSA: Again, it would depend on your alternatives. I think that kind of success against your pitcher is going to mean the hitter has a legitimate psychological edge. He knows he's having that kind of success, and that makes him more confident. The pitcher knows he has been giving that hitter a lot to hit but sometimes, no matter how hard he tries, he only makes things worse. So. if you had another reliever that you could go to, I probably would make a change. The other thing, though, you may not always be able to switch pitchers. So, one thing you can do when you have a pitcher who's having trouble with hitters is to pitch that hitter very tough. What you can give him is a very uncomfortable at bat. Every pitch that he throws is like 0-2, so usually the hitter is very aggressive and might get himself out. However, if he doesn't and the pitcher walks him, it's better than just throwing the ball down the middle.

JOE BUCK: Okay, Tony La Russa, here's today's question. A pitcher's having a bad inning but he's scheduled to lead off the next one. How do you decide whether to take him out or to leave him in?

TONY LA RUSSA: There are some important considerations in just about any direction you go, but to me, it's a good example of when you have to keep your priorities in order, and one of the major priorities you have is to play the inning you're involved in. You don't want to get caught too much in looking too far ahead. In that particular inning, while you're waiting to have him get through the inning so you don't waste an extra hitter or pitcher, the game may evaporate before your eyes. So, I think normally you want to try to limit the damage in the inning you're playing. You may face a situation in which you're really short on the bench or in the bullpen, and you have to push that pitcher a little farther, but that's

GAME DECISIONS

the risk you take. Normally, I would try to stop the damage in the inning you're playing.

JOE BUCK: Okay, Tony La Russa, here's today's question. Your starter has a big lead but he's having trouble in the ninth inning. How difficult is it for that pitcher to talk you into letting him stay in and try to finish the ballgame?

TONY LA RUSSA: One of the things you learn is: Very seldom do you walk to the mound and ask a pitcher how he feels, because they're always going to be heroes. They're in the middle of the competition, and their adrenaline is pumping. They're always going to give you the answer that says they want to keep pitching: "Hey, I feel fine." What you want to do is look at the game, evaluate the pitcher, and make your decision before you go out there. So, rarely do you ask a pitcher and give him a chance to talk you out of it. Most of the time, managers will tell you that they don't even want any conversation. I hold out my hand, and the pitcher places the ball in it. Once in a while, if you have a pitcher who's very experienced and you really trust him, you go out there and ask him a question if you know he'll use good sense. However, you normally make your decision before you go to the mound.

JOE BUCK: Okay, Tony, here's today's question. It's the ninth inning, your starter's throwing the ball well but he's thrown a lot of pitches. How do you decide whether to leave him in or put in a reliever?

TONY LA RUSSA: You look at several factors, and that is one of your toughest calls, because if your starter has pitched very well through eight innings, that's an indication he may be the best guy for the ninth inning. You never know, no matter how good your closer is, on that particular day what he's going to throw, but you have the ability to watch your starter who has been pitching. I think the number of pitches is a good indication. You don't want to do something for one game that jeopardizes his whole career or the

GAME DECISIONS

rest of the season, so with every pitcher you'll get a range of pitches where it becomes very dangerous to let him continue. To me, dangerous means two things. It could be dangerous because he could hurt himself. If you stress an arm and really reach for that little extra when you're fatigued, that's how you can blow arms out. The second thing is: It's dangerous because you put the game in jeopardy as you start to get tired, and you reach for extra when it's just not there. That same breaking ball that's been snapping starts rolling, and that same fastball that's been located perfectly starts getting more towards the middle or dangerous areas for hitters. I think you really watch the pitchers, you try to look for any difference in their pitches, and their pitch count is an important determinant.

JOE BUCK: How does an outfielder decide which base to throw to? Particularly when there's a runner going to home or third and another rounding first?

TONY LA RUSSA: This involves one of the most important drills that you work your outfielders with during spring training. It's one of those plays, in the course of a game, that many times gets overlooked. The significance can really turn around and bite you. What we usually teach is: Hit the cutoff man; that's your number one responsibility, and that will stop the runners to a certain extent. The other thing that we try to teach: How often do you see a runner thrown out at home or third if your outfielder has to go side to side? Normally, one of our keys is, if an outfielder moves left or right to pick up the base hit, instead of making that throw to the cutoff man, he goes ahead and throws to second base. Keep the double play in order. More big innings are turned against you because the outfielder will try to make this heroic play and make this heave all the way to the cutoff man, or to the plate or third. The hitter, instead of being on first, goes to second. The next play is a little ground ball that would have got you out of the inning but turns out to extend the inning for another run or two. So we usually teach: If it's right at you, make the play — hit the cutoff man. If you have to go side to side, just throw the ball to second and keep the double play in order.

GAME DECISIONS

JOE BUCK: Now, Tony La Russa, here's today baseball question. Often a reliever comes into the game and intentionally walks the first batter. That would seem a negative way to start. Why don't managers have the previous pitcher give up the walk before bringing in the new guy?

TONY LA RUSSA: I would probably quarrel with the word "often" in that question, Joe. Most of the time managers, for the obvious reason the question is bringing up, want the reliever to come in and throw strikes. He's been throwing strikes in the bullpen and you want him to come out right away trying to get out the first hitter he faces. You don't want to force him to throw four pitches off the plate. However, there is one strategy you may have to use. Every time you bring in a pitcher from the bullpen, he must face at least one batter before he can be replaced. Sometimes, to qualify him as an appearance in the ball game, you do bring in the reliever, and he serves up the intentional walk. That allows you, in case the manager on the other side wants to pinch-hit for the next guy, to make another pitching change if you want. If you bring in the reliever and he's going to have to pitch to the first hitter he faces, the other manager can always set up the match-up that he wants, and you can't ever play around that situation.

JOE BUCK: When play resumes after a lengthy rain delay, how do you decide to continue to use the same pitcher or to make a change?

TONY LA RUSSA: I think one of the key factors in that question is the word "lengthy." Lengthy would mean you definitely tend to favor removing the pitcher and going to somebody else. If you think about the initial warm-up he has, that's a 10 to 15 minute process, and then you get into the game. When you have to shut it down for a long period of time, you're asking him to start the warm-up all over again. It's usually very dangerous. I think the factor you would look at, though, is that some pitchers are stronger, their arms are in better shape, or maybe the guy has been a little "ouchy" in his elbow or his shoulder and you wouldn't

GAME DECISIONS

want to push. So you look at the circumstances. You may look at the kind of game he's having. If he's really been cruising, you can see that he's in a great mechanical shape that day, and the pitches are being released effortlessly, you may want to send him back out there. However, lengthy usually means it's dangerous to send a guy back out there for a second warm-up.

JOE BUCK: There's no score in the third inning. The Cardinals have runners on first and second with nobody out. Your pitcher is trying to lay down a bunt, but he's fouled two off and has two strikes. Do you still have him bunting with two strikes?

TONY LA RUSSA: Very often you do, because if you let him swing, typically he is not one of the best hitters on the ball club. If you let him swing, he's liable to hit a little roller to one of the infielders, which turns into a double play. They usually aren't the best runners on the team either, so by letting him swing in that situation it may turn into a double play. Then you're left with a runner on third and two outs. If you bunt and he fouls it off, at least you still have first and second with one out. You've got a chance for a bigger inning with your first and second guy coming up. I think one of the other factors you look at is to really work on the pitcher's bunting. For example, last year's Cardinal club was really high up in the league as far as number of attempts and successes. I think a lot goes into the work that's done in spring training right through the season. However, there's no doubt in my mind that, if your bunter is fundamentally sound and he's the pitcher, in that great of a scoring situation — first and second with nobody out — you're probably going to take three chances to advance those runners.

JOE BUCK: Is it ever a good idea to play the infield in early in the game?

TONY LA RUSSA: Absolutely. In fact, I think this, along with not playing the line, are two of the baseball bible chapters that have been messed with the most in the last 10 to 15 years that I've been

GAME DECISIONS

managing. I think you don't see the line protected as often, and you see the infield brought in early much more often than it is held back. To me, the thinking I've been taught is: You try to figure out how costly is that run at third base? How much can you afford to let it score? Compare that against trying to prevent the run. If you bring the infield in, do you open yourself up for a big inning? Theoretically, you improve the hitter's chance to get on base with a blooper or some type of ground ball that gets through, and trying to save that one run may instead lead to two or three or four. That's why I look at the speed of the runner, what our chances are to have a big-scoring game or a close-scoring game, and the type of hitter. If it's someone like Delino DeShields or Kenny Lofton who's at the plate, and you let him get on base with this little ground ball that snuck through, he may turn that into a steal and then another steal, so that one run turns into two or three. You look at all those things. If you expect a close game, play the infield in early.

JOE BUCK: Now, Tony La Russa, here's today's question. Some managers call pitches from the dugout. Others leave pitch selection to the catcher. Which system do you use and why?

TONY LA RUSSA: We definitely prefer to have the catcher run the game. The biggest problem with calling pitches from the dugout is you're not really into the flow. By that I mean, the flow is basically sixty feet away from the pitcher — you watch his telltale signs of excitement, fatigue, and all these things. From the dugout, you have a feel for it, but you're not as close to it as a catcher. More importantly, you're not catching his pitches, which is the best telltale of all. So what we like to do is prepare our catcher before the game. Dave Duncan meets every day with our catcher, and they talk about our pitcher versus their hitters. What the catcher can always do is glance to the dugout if he's ever stumped, and Dunc or myself will give a suggestion about what we would call on this situation. However, it's much better to prepare the catcher and let him react to the differences.

GAME DECISIONS

JOE BUCK: Your pitcher has been doing well, but he's been out there for awhile. What things do you look for to determine if he's getting tired and ready to be pulled?

TONY LA RUSSA: This is one area in which you have to be willing to make the move before the big damage. There's a big priority in getting to know your pitchers, establishing honest communication, and having a catcher who's willing to stand up and take some responsibility by saying, "Hey, his stuff is starting to really back off," because you may not be able to see it from the dugout. The factors you do look at, if you watch closely from the beginning of the game, you will see the type of mechanics and the type of stuff that he has. When you start to see the pitches change in a negative way, that's an indication. For example, if a fastball has been looking like this and all of sudden it looks like it's less, or if a breaking ball has been snapping sharply and all of a sudden it starts rolling. If you see a guy who has been in command of himself and starts missing his pitches, this is an indication of fatigue. Body language — in which you can see a guy when he is fresh, and you can see a guy when he's starting to get tired and starting to get frustrated — factors into making the move. I think the biggest problem is: Anytime a pitcher gives up the damage, and you make the move after the runs have been scored, then that's the quickest way to lose a game and lose your job. You have to be ready to anticipate the move when those telltale signs first show up.

JOE BUCK: The Cardinals have a man on first base with one out. What figures into your decision whether to send the runner to avoid a ground ball double play?

TONY LA RUSSA: There's a couple of ways to look at this question. One, is it before the hitter has three balls, or is it during other parts of the count? I think one of the most important factors you look at is: If it's less than the three-ball count, does your runner have any chance to steal that base if the ball does get to the catcher? Yes, you can anticipate a ground ball based on the type of hitter you've got and the pitcher you are facing. You know if a

GAME DECISIONS

ground ball comes, it could wipe out the inning with a double play. But, how can you foil that? You could play hit-and-run, for example, or you might make a steal attempt. You would really have to evaluate if that runner has a chance to steal the base. This would depend on his speed and the pitcher's unloading time, but would depend very little on the catcher's throwing ability. Finally, if it's a three-ball count with less than two outs, do you send him 3-1, or do you send him 3-2? There's a lot riding, here again, on the type of hitter and the type of pitcher. If he's a big strikeout pitcher, a strikeout hitter, and the guy doesn't run very well, then you may be running yourself right out of an inning, just like a double play with a ground ball. If you've got something going for you, my general rule is: When in doubt, be aggressive.

JOE BUCK: The Cardinals have a runner on third with less than two outs. The batter hits a ground ball. How does the runner decide to go home or stay at third?

TONY LA RUSSA: The way he decides is one of the responsibilities of the bench or the manager. The manager will flash a sign to the third base coach that will tell the third base coach to either make the ball go through or go on contact. "Go on contact" means he tries to get a running jump, so as soon as the ball is put into play, he runs home. How do you decide which of those two to do? If it's less than two outs, obviously if there's nobody out, you would more than likely try to make the ball go through. This is because you would hate to run into an out at the plate and lose a great chance to score from third base with less than two outs. If there is a runner on third with one out, you would more often try to play contact. Here's a version of this play that is very good, and you can get the best of both worlds: You can have that runner break on contact with one out almost all of the time. From the minute he sees the ground ball was hit close enough to an infielder that there's going to be a play at the plate and he's going to be out easily - he stops. He gets into a rundown, and if your hitter is hustling he can round first and get to second. The runner at third is tagged out, but you've got the runner at second

GAME DECISIONS

with two outs and in scoring position for a base hit. You've also picked up the chance to score him if that contact play works, and the ground ball had to make an infielder move left to right.

JOE BUCK: **What factors go into deciding whether to attempt to steal third base, and would you ever try it with a left hander on the plate?**

TONY LA RUSSA: I'll take the back half of that question first. Yes, I would definitely try it with a left-hander at bat, because the single most important factor you look at is the unloading time or the release time of the pitcher. If the pitcher is very deliberate to the plate, you can steal third even with a left-handed hitter. But that is a good point in the question. Normally, with the left-handed hitter, the catcher has the wide-open view of the runner going and the easy step to third base. It's very easy to make that throw, so you really have to factor that into your attempt. However, the factors you look at are how slow the pitcher is unloading the pitch to the plate, and then you look at where your middle infielders are. One of the players, second or short, will have the coverage responsibility, and you try to see how much attention he's paying to the runner. Finally, defenses will frequently back up with two outs. I think it's a good base to take with two outs, because there are so many ways to score from third base, such as a wild pitch, an infield hit or an error. So it is a bag to steal, but with two outs, you want to make sure you can make it and not take any chances.

JOE BUCK: **Tony, your top starter has a no-hitter going with a one run lead in the bottom of the ninth inning. Their best hitter is coming up with two outs and a runner at second base. Do you stick with the starter and get caught up in all of the emotion, or do you worry about the end result of the game and bring somebody else in?**

TONY LA RUSSA: There's no doubt in my mind the most difficult situation for a manager is the one that is described in this question, because you have all the tough considerations. You have

GAME DECISIONS

a one run lead, so you have no margin for mistake. If you wrongly evaluate whether the pitcher's still got his stuff enough to get the out, if you make a mistake, you're going to contribute to losing the game. Then you have that other consideration. If a pitcher has gone into the ninth inning — here it's the extreme; you're talking about a no hitter, so obviously he's very dominant that particular day. But usually the question is more that he has a low-hit game going, and he's winning 2-1 or 1-0, meaning he's been pitching very, very well all game long. You start to really watch him in the seventh, eighth and ninth to see when fatigue starts to be a factor. However, if he has that kind of dominance, the other side has a little moral deficit against that pitcher, and if you go to your reliever, most of the time it picks up the offense, because they're seeing somebody new and they get a fresh start. So usually you stay with a starter if he's got that kind of great game going.

JOE BUCK: **Tony, when you go to your bullpen, how do you decide which reliever to use in a certain situation?**

TONY LA RUSSA: That's one of the toughest decisions a manager makes, and I think one of the biggest contributions a manager can make to the team. The game is really played by your players on the field for both sides, but as manager and a coach, you can contribute a decision, evaluate pitching, and decide who's the best match-up for your club to give you the best chance to win. I think that's one of your biggest challenges. What I think happens too much sometimes — especially now with so much statistical help from which you can receive percentages and find out who has success or failure against a certain player — you go too much with a formula. So what we try to do is to make sure we understand what the history is between pitchers and hitters. However, in a particular situation, you want to look at who's been hot in your bullpen, who is rested, and at what part of the game. You also want to look beyond that inning, because you're going to have to get some outs after it. You want to look at who their bullpen is. Sometimes, for example, you may have a left-handed hitter who hits the ball up, and you have a left-handed reliever who makes

GAME DECISIONS

breaking ball mistakes up. You may want to go to a right-hander who has a sinker ball, because he's more likely to get the ball down and away, which is the out area for that particular hitter. So to me, that's one of the great challenges to try and figure out: The hitter, your pitcher's strength, and put together the rest or fatigue factor.

JOE BUCK: Tony, when your pitching coach goes to the mound, predominantly, what is he out there to say to his pitcher?

TONY LA RUSSA: I think you try to use common sense, and I think fans can, a lot of times, guess or figure out along with the pitching coach what he's going to talk about, and they'll be accurate. For example, if you see a pitcher who's flustered, you can just see that emotion has added to his problem. Maybe he's getting beat around a little bit, and you start to see him getting dejected or get too excited; the pitching coach is going to go out there and talk about emotions and attitude. If you look at somebody who is suddenly in a bad groove, and his pitches are not as effective as they were, and you see something mechanical, a quick trip to the mound is just to correct his mechanical keys. One of these mechanical keys is very often rushing. For example, where you don't let your arm go high enough and get through your delivery. The pitching coach will go out there and say something about the mechanics. Finally, there is a time where it is just the strategy. It's a tense part of the game and you want to be sure the intelligent thing is attempted, you bring the pitcher and catcher together. You talk about the hitter and about the situation they're facing. You want to be sure that they're thinking the right things: Let's really go after this guy, let's not give into this guy, let's pitch around him, and what is the pitch we're going to try that gives us our best chance in this situation.

GAME DECISIONS

JOE BUCK: Tony, presumably your closer is the relief pitcher you want pitching when the game is on the line, but what if the game is on the line before the ninth inning? Let's say bases loaded or a couple men on with a small lead in the seventh or eighth inning. Do you bring your closer in then or do you keep him down in your bullpen for later?

TONY LA RUSSA: This is the question and the argument you get a lot for managers like myself, who usually save the closer for the ninth inning. And my answer would be: Obviously, if this is a key moment in the game, it makes some sense to bring in your closer to get that out in the seventh inning. However, then what do you do in the eighth? Let's just carry it a little bit. If you let this guy pitch the eighth and the ninth, do you know how many days it's going to be before he's available to pitch again? That's really the theory most of us use. The more times a closer can be available, the more chances you have to win. So you must limit the number of outs he gets. If you were going to pitch him in the seventh, then you have to have confidence that somebody else can come in the eighth and ninth and close out the game. However, that usually isn't the case. If you were going to pitch him in the seventh and let him finish the rest of the game, you're going to lose him for several days. So my answer is: Only very occasionally would you feel the game is so important at that point that you would risk the closer. Remember, you still have six outs of your own to make more runs.

JOE BUCK: Tony, let's say it's late in a low-scoring, tie game. The other team has runners in scoring position, and one of their better hitters coming up. Do you bring your closer in then to stop the rally, or save him in case the game goes extra innings?

TONY LA RUSSA: There are two keys there: One is said and one is going to have to be assumed. One key is a tie game, and that presents a whole different set of circumstances if you're thinking about your bullpen. A tie means you still don't have the win in hand; you're not ahead. So if the closer gets the out, you've got a

GAME DECISIONS

better chance to win, but you're still going to have to do something to score. The other point you want to consider: Are you talking about a road game or at home? Anytime you have a tie game on the road, and you use the closer to get out of that inning in the ninth, you have to score in the top of the tenth. The closer has to come back and pitch the bottom of the tenth. Very often, the opposite is true. If you're at home, you have a tie game in the ninth inning, you can bring your closer in to get out of the top of the ninth and you will insure yourself of at least six outs to win that game. You'll bat in the bottom of the ninth. Maybe he goes out or somebody else goes out in the top of the tenth, and you will always hit in the bottom of the tenth. So, I would definitely think about using a closer if it's a tie game at home, eighth or ninth inning. I would very rarely try to do it on the road.

JOE BUCK: Tony, in the middle innings of a close game, your starting pitcher is coming to bat. How do you decide whether to let him hit or pinch hit for him and then go to your bullpen?

TONY LA RUSSA: There are certain things to look for. If the question is "a close game," is that a close game 6-5 or is it 2-1? Six-to-five means he's toiled and hasn't had a great day. He's been competitive, but there is no reason to think that he's going to blank them from here to the end, since he hasn't done it so far. If it's 2-1, now he's pitched very effectively, you are just in the middle, and you have a lot of outs left to get. I would think most of the time you're going to want to let him continue to pitch, because he's proven he's effective that day. The other consideration would be: Just exactly where the rally is at that point. If you've got a chance to blow that game open — perhaps the bases are loaded with one out and you feel like your bullpen is rested and ready to go — then you might want to pinch-hit for him and take a chance of putting the game out of reach. If he's coming up and nothing is happening, I would almost certainly, if he's pitching well, stay with your pitcher and save the bullpen for later.

GAME DECISIONS

JOE BUCK: Tony, how and when do you decide to have a relief pitcher start throwing in your bullpen?

TONY LA RUSSA: I think this is probably one of the biggest mistakes a young manager, and even the old managers like me, make. You will get so concerned about what's happening on the field, you start thinking ahead as to what is the worse thing that can happen. That's when the team hitting against you is able to get a rally going, and you're not able to counter. You'll call the bullpen just to get activity and be ready, in case the stuff starts to really go against you. You have to really remind yourself that, every time a reliever gets up to throw, it takes something away from him. There is a golden rule, if you can do this, to not have your reliever up unless you really think he is going to pitch in that game, or is likely to pitch in that game. So the way you work around that sometimes is to have several stages of getting a reliever loose. If it's cold, maybe you just have him up playing catch, because just playing catch isn't going to take a lot away from him. Then we have another one in which we just have him go halfway. In other words, he goes a little farther, but he's not really cutting loose. You can do the getting loose and the halfway two or three times without worrying about the pitcher losing his stuff and getting stiff. However, you want to be careful about getting the pitcher ready unless you know he's going to pitch in the game.

JOE BUCK: Tony, late in the game you lead by one, but your opponent has the bases loaded with one out. Do you bring in all four infielders for a play at the plate or do you keep the shortstop and second baseman back to try for that inning-ending double play?

TONY LA RUSSA: There are several considerations. One I would think about is: Are you at home or on the road? For example, you're on the road and you have a chance to win the game. You may want to shoot the works, because usually, unless you've got the much better club and much better bullpen, it's tougher to win

GAME DECISIONS

a game late after the score is tied and you go into extra innings. At home, you may want to be a little bit more conservative, and make sure the game doesn't get away from you. If you think about it, if the bases are loaded and you play the infield in, a ground ball that gets through will mean not just that you're tied but you'll be behind by a run. I think the most important factor you look at is the combination of the speed of the runner at third and, especially, the speed of the hitter at the plate. If the hitter at the plate is a very good double play candidate, you'll go to double play depth, because almost any ground ball he hits you can turn into a double play if the infielder can catch it. Also, playing back means you're going to increase the range of the infielders. If the guy at the plate, though, is a real speed burner, then you're forced to play the infield in, because if he hits a ground ball, you will not turn a double play, and your most important consideration there is to cut off the tying run at the plate.

JOE BUCK: Tony, when you bring the infield in you take the chance, always, that a hard-hit ball might go through and lead to a bigger inning. How do you weigh those possibilities, and what's your overall feeling on bringing the infield in?

TONY LA RUSSA: That's another one baseball people would argue about. Actually, the way the question is phrased, the hard-hit ball, you don't worry as much about the hard-hit ball if it gets through. Veteran infielders — and I've been around some great ones like Doug Rader and Eddie Brinkman who were very good major league infielders — talk about the triangle effect. With coming in and going back, you really don't increase or decrease your range very much. As you go back, the triangle effect means you cover a little more ground but you don't really lose much, as far as range. I worry a lot more about the blooper — the little pop fly that would have been an easy out for somebody had they been playing back but that somehow gets over the infield. So to me, playing the infield "in" used to be by the book. You never did it until the last three innings of the game, but more and more you see guys do it early. Don Baylor, for one, always goes against

GAME DECISIONS

convention, because he will do it early in the game in Colorado where a lot of runs are going to be scored. Normally, the only time you play the infield in early is if you think it's going to be a low scoring game, and every run will be precious.

JOE BUCK: **Tony, when a game turns into a blowout, how soon do you use your bench to give them some work and rest your regulars?**

TONY LA RUSSA: It really depends on whose blowout it is. If it's a blowout against you, I think the sooner you get your regulars out of there, very often, the better. You save them the wear and tear and agony of a bad day. It could be the fifth or sixth inning, and you're really getting killed, 10-0 for example, and you need these players game in, game out, month in, month out. So if you take them out, you save them from having to toil through a really tough day. Plus there's another strategy: Very often, since it's not working with that unit, you bring in fresh blood off the bench, and these extra guys that particular day will come in with a lot of energy and will get several base hits. I've seen games reversed by going to the bench early. The opposite's true, though, if you've got a blowout in your favor. You never want to assume too early that the game is in hand. Once you start pulling regulars, you're going to start playing a little shorter. It might seem like you're insulting the other club. They get a little motivated, they get something going, and you can't stem the tide because you have no reserves left. So you need to be very careful when you get the lead in hand, but it's okay when the lead is against you. I think the other thing is: You want to consider the ballpark and the chance that a lot of runs will be scored that particular day.

GAME DECISIONS

JOE BUCK: Tony, with a runner on third base, what factors have to be present for you to call or even contemplate a suicide squeeze?

TONY LA RUSSA: I think, unfortunately, a suicide squeeze is one of those things that, if you have a situation where you don't have a hitter who you're very confident can drive the runner in, everybody knows it. Fans know it, and the other side definitely knows it. One factor is the ability of the hitter to produce the run. Then, when you get into a situation where the hitter is not very dangerous, you look at the other factors. Since everybody is looking for it, what really increases your chances to get a successful pitch and a squeeze down? The obvious points to look at are the types of pitchers. Is he somebody who's around the plate? Is he very wild? You would much rather try to squeeze against a sinker-baller than a high fast ball pitcher, because you'll pop it up, perhaps pop into a double play. The other real key — and most managers will tell you this in a clinic, for example - is you try to get the other side in a situation where they have to throw a strike. Then you try to squeeze on that particular one. Occasionally, though, you can be so out of the ordinary, like a 0-1 count for example, which is usually a time that a pitcher can nibble a little bit. You put it on because they won't expect you to try to do it in that situation. It's really a guessing game.

JOE BUCK: Tony, there's a fast runner on first with a couple of outs and a weak-hitting pitcher at the plate. Is it a good or bad idea to try to have that runner steal second?

TONY LA RUSSA: That's a great question, because the obvious answer is you don't want to run yourself out of an inning and have that weak-hitting pitcher lead off the top of the next inning. That's just going to start that inning with an out. Most of the time, what you're thinking is: Don't run, and make sure the pitcher gets his chance to swing so you can start fresh the next inning with a leadoff guy. As soon as I say that, since there was such an emphasis on our club to, if we can, have legs in the eighth spot,

GAME DECISIONS

you will face pitchers that are giving you that stolen base. The best example I can use here is Royce Clayton. When he hits eighth, he is an excellent base stealer and has excellent legs. You'll get a pitcher on the mound who has a slow release, and a catcher who may not throw that great. It's a high-percentage play to send him. Is it a good baseball play? Probably not, because if he stumbles and gets thrown out, you'll be kicking yourself. However, I think you want to stay aggressive whenever possible. If that stolen base is there, then that weak-hitting pitcher just might bloop one to right field for a hit. So generally, you want to shut down your running game. But if it's there, and it's a gift, go ahead and take it because perhaps the guy will run into a mistake.

JOE BUCK: **Tony, if you want to advance a runner, do you have your batter try to hit the ball to the right side of the infield, hit-and-run, run-and-hit, or do you just go ahead and bunt?**

TONY LA RUSSA: All of the above; I think that's the answer. It really depends on your hitter. Obviously, if you want to be aggressive and you count all 27 outs as precious, the more you have a runner on second and you let your hitter at the plate swing away, you're not just giving up the out. That makes a lot of sense if the hitter has a chance to hit the ball to the right side and get a base hit. If he's just going to push the ball to the right side without much chance of hitting with authority, or if he has trouble hitting it to the right side, then you're going to look at the next option. So, first option: Love for him to swing the bat and maybe get a base hit and not give up an out. However, if there's any doubt, it's a big run if the guy gets to third base with one out, and you're really thinking you can score the run, great chance to score, then you start looking at the other options. Hit-and-run, I like a lot because it's an aggressive play, if the guy at bat can put the ball in play and the pitcher is not too wild. If any of those factors are not there for you, then I think the bunt is the right strategy, because the runner at third is a run-scoring opportunity, and you don't want to miss advancing him if you can help it.

GAME DECISIONS

JOE BUCK: Tony, in what situations might you try a double steal?

TONY LA RUSSA: There are a couple of different double steals. There is the first and second, where you'd go for second and third. The other one is more dramatic, which is first and third, where the guy on first steals second and on the throw through the runner on third tries to steal home. The first one you see quite a bit; in fact, you'll see it a lot with the Cardinals. First and second is an RBI situation; so very often, especially with two outs, you'll see the defenders move back to take away the base hit, and all of a sudden your runners can get another two or three steps. I like the double steal with two outs, because if you think about it, if they successfully steal, a base hit is two runs, not one. So we will look at the double steal with runners on first and second. We're always looking for it if we have runners with legs, and it's always depending on how quick the pitcher unloads and how much attention the middle infielder is giving the runner at second. The double steal with runners on first and third — this is a tougher one. This is because you really have to expect that you've got their strategy figured out, and you know the throw is going to go through. If you execute properly, and the runner breaks correctly, if the ball is thrown and the runner breaks, he should be able to score from third to home, and the runner on first stops. However, you have to know the ball is going through from the catcher.

JOE BUCK: Tony, is it ever too early in a game to lay down a sacrifice bunt?

TONY LA RUSSA: Absolutely not. I think that, here again, it's a way to make the point about strategy just being a matter of opinion. You watch a game, and your opinion might be different than mine. However, I've seen some very successful managers: I remember Jim Leyland about '92 or '93 always bunted with Jay Bell in the first inning to get the lead, and they ended up winning their division and going up against the Braves. I don't often bunt with the second-place hitter to get the runner to second. Normally you try to do something more aggressive. Normally, if you have a

GAME DECISIONS

hitter who can do something; it doesn't just give up the out. What you'll see me do with a leadoff double, if I'm not sure the hitter at the bat can get the runner to third base, I will sacrifice in that situation with the runner on second and the guy at bat with nobody out. To me, what you're saying there is: The value of one run in the game depends on the way you smell that particular game. If you think it's going to be a low-scoring game, then you don't want to miss your best chance to score that run, which would be to advance the guy on base with the bunt. I think: Rarely from first to second, more often from second to third, and only if you think it's going to be a low scoring game.

JOE BUCK: Tony, some hitters like to be aggressive in first-pitch, fast ball situations. Is that always a good idea?

TONY LA RUSSA: One of the real dilemmas is in hitting. You talk to Ted Williams, and Ted will say it's a very good idea to watch a pitcher's stuff. Don't worry about getting the count. The more confident a guy is the more he understands that, if he gets deeper in the count, he sees more pitches, and he can still save the at bat. However, I think the general rule for most hitters who don't have Ted Williams' or Wade Boggs' kind of ability, is they should be ready to hit the first pitch they see that's in a good spot and they can put a good swing on. Too often, if a guy makes a first pitch out, and you start getting on him about it, he will start taking the first pitch. It might be the best pitch he had to hit the whole at bat; and now he's just not to be too aggressive and he'll back off it. So what we try to teach is: Be ready to swing as soon as you go to bat, but be selective early in the count. Don't offer at the pitch unless it's really in your happy zone. If it is, be ready to swing and be aggressive. If it isn't — if they throw a ball in the outside corner and you're looking middle in — take that pitch, and work the count some. It really comes down to being aggressive, but only with something you know you can drive if you get that particular pitch.

GAME DECISIONS

JOE BUCK: **Tony, in a blowout in your team's favor, how quickly would you be tempted to pull the starting pitcher to save his arm for the next start?**

TONY LA RUSSA: I think you put a few factors together. Number one, you love that situation. It doesn't happen nearly enough. But you want to consider your bullpen. I think a lot has to do with that bullpen. If it's one that has really been taxed lately, then you probably want to push your starter a little farther. That's because you're going to play another game the next day, and you may not have the blowout game, so you're going to need your bullpen. If the bullpen is rested, then that's the best situation. Any time you can save your starter pitches — especially if he is one of your main guys and is going to go out there thirty plus times in a year — any time you have one of these games and you can save him an inning, that's 10, 15 or 18 pitches. So that will mean he has those extra pitches for you the next time he goes out there. In a blowout game, you always want to think about him pitching at least six innings; but that still leaves nine outs for your bullpen, and you want to carefully consider whether those nine outs would be good for your bullpen. Is there somebody who needs the work? If they've been pitching a lot, then you probably want to get your starter through the seventh. I would rarely pitch a starter more than seven in a blowout game.

JOE BUCK: **Tony, what factors go into deciding to let a hitter hit away with a count of three balls, no strikes?**

TONY LA RUSSA: There is a lot that has to do with the hitter himself and the opportunities you give him. If you give a hitter a 3-0 hit, and in his first few chances he takes a swing even if the ball isn't thrown anywhere in the vicinity of the plate, you're less likely to ever let him do it again. The idea is that he's in a great position to hit. The pitcher has got three strikes he has to throw to him, so with the 3-0, you should really make it a small area where he knows that, if the ball goes there, he's going to put his best swing and make very good contact. If he shows that kind of discipline, you're likely to do it. The other thing is the power of the hitter. If

GAME DECISIONS

he's just a singles hitter and you let him have that big chance to swing, and the most damage he's going to do is a little line drive, you're better off, percentage-wise, on trying to make the pitcher throw three strikes, because he may hit the ball hard right at somebody. If the hitter has legitimate extra-base pop, he's more dangerous and more likely to let swing 3-0. I think it's the other situation that comes up a lot. With runners in scoring position, and I don't care who the hitter is, if the guy is showing he's got some judgment and some selectivity, you let him swing, single or extra base, because he's in charge and a base hit will produce runs.

JOE BUCK: Tony, late in a game on the road, do you play for a tie and hope to win it in extra innings, or do you try to get that lead, hold on to it and win the game?

TONY LA RUSSA: It's a judgment call. I think the general rule would be: On the road you try to get the lead and hold onto it. It's very difficult to win a tie game on the road, because the other side has that extra at bat. If you score in the top of the tenth, they get to hit in the bottom of the tenth. If the score is tied, and they score in their bottom of the inning, the game is over. Usually, you play the road game to win and you don't play to tie. What's the exception? I think if you feel like you've really got the other side overmatched, then the longer you play with them, the better chance you have to win. So you may not want to take any unnecessary risks when you've got a game tied, because you're thinking, "If we play long enough, we're so much better than the other club, we'll find a way to beat them." One of those places where you make that evaluation is if the other club has a bad bullpen. I think more games are decided in extra innings by the quality of the bullpen than the quality of the clutch hitting on either side. If you think you can score against the other side's bullpen, then keep it close or keep it tied, because sooner or later you'll break through. If you're worried about your bullpen, vice versa, then you need to try to win as quick as you can, because you know your reliever's going to give it up. So, with a good bullpen on the road, you should try to go for it.

GAME DECISIONS

JOE BUCK: Tony, tie game. The other team has a fast runner on first base, and you think he is going to steal. If the count is already 2-0, do you dare pitchout?

TONY LA RUSSA: I think you do. It's not a common practice, but you've got to think about the disadvantage. If they already have a fast runner on first base and the hitter's got a 2-0 count, they've already got a lot of things going for them that could produce a big inning. One thing you could do, if you guess right and they're running, is to throw the guy out. The count's 3-0 now, but at least you've got one out. I think you really want to look at how certain you are the guy is running. You also want to consider, if the guy's very fast, you may be able to pitchout correctly and still not throw him out. However, I don't think it's the worst move you can make, because you're facing a very tough, run-scoring chance there. With the hitter at 2-0 and a fast runner on first, that offensive side against you has so many ways to score that run, or more importantly, break that inning open. That's what I would be worrying about. I would be worrying about that becoming a big inning. It may be a time where you would want to follow the old saying, "No guts, no glory." Better to try to throw out a runner stealing, so you can get an out and take the sting out of the inning. If you go first and second with nobody out, you're still facing trouble.

JOE BUCK: Tony, with a runner on third base and less than two outs, what determines if you'll send that runner when the hitter makes contact?

TONY LA RUSSA: This is one of the great situations in baseball, Joe. I have a lot of fun with it. I think it's one of the crucial calls that you make, and one of the considerations is the speed of the runner at third. If the guy's not a good runner, he's going to take too long to get to the plate so you can't make that play work. If the runner has very good speed, then we really can make this play. I'll knock on wood that we can live up to this, but we have several guys who run well and get great breaks. In the two years I've been here, we really make the contact play right. We have guys like Brian, Ray,

GAME DECISIONS

Delino, who I say have rolling leads. Ron and all these guys really get great jumps, so speed is good. You also want to look at the type of surface. Sometimes on turf, the ball gets to the infielders so quick, you may not want to send the runner. However, you may want to read a chop and send him. Besides, I think the most important factor is: Who is the hitter on deck? If you think the guy on deck has a very good chance to get a base hit, then you may not want to risk losing that hitter in scoring position, so you'll hold him. Finally, there is one "cover your butt" way. If you do send him on contact, and if he's thrown out at the plate, he can stop and get caught in a rundown. Then the hitter should be able to round the base, get to second, and you still have a guy in scoring position for that next hitter with two outs.

JOE BUCK: Tony, when you make a double switch to bring in a relief pitcher, how do you decide which position player to take out of the game?

TONY LA RUSSA: I think the most obvious answer is: The player who most recently made an out, because then you would stretch out the time between when your pitcher spot comes up again in the batting order. If the seventh-place hitter made an out, and you want to switch it, you may go for the seventh place. However, there are other factors that come into your consideration. That player you're thinking about who is the most recent out could also be one of your key RBI producers, or a player who, defensively, you can't really replace from off the bench. So then you go to the next best choice. Sometimes you try to get a little cuter. Let's say you really just want your pitcher to pitch an inning, and it also works out that the best guy to substitute — the deepest place on your bench — is four or five hitters away. You could insure — and I've done this with Willie McGee before — you can insure that Willie McGee comes up to pinch hit the next inning by putting the pitcher in three or four spots ahead. So, it's not always the guy that made the last out. I think you use other considerations, such as who's on your bench, how long are your pitcher and relief pitcher

GAME DECISIONS

going to pitch, and who is going to come into play, as to who is really a hitter that you would like to send up there in the next inning.

JOE BUCK: Tony, top of the eighth, one out, and the Cardinals are winning 3-1 with runners on second and third. A batter like Mike Piazza is due up. Would you walk him to set up the double play, even though it means putting the winning run on base, or would you pitch to him?

TONY LA RUSSA: There are several factors here. Number one, when you mention somebody like Mike Piazza, you're talking about one of the most dangerous hitters in Major League baseball. So, one of the factors is: Just how dangerous is that hitter? Normally, you go into a game against a lineup, and there are one or two guys that you fear the most that particular day, such as Piazza, against all your pitchers. It could be one guy who's really tough against your pitcher that day. So, if you have that very dangerous hitter, a good strategy is to try to play that game without letting that guy beat you. The way you do this is take the bat out of his hands as often as you can. In that situation, I probably would walk Piazza, even though it's the winning run. Normally, when you intentionally walk a guy, it's because you think you pick up a substantial edge against the player that you're going to bring to bat instead of the hitter that you're walking. The other thing you really want to consider, and this is where you've got to be really careful, is any time you walk the bases loaded, you're making it very tough for your pitcher. You're making it very easy for the hitter, because he knows the ball has to be thrown over the plate.

JOE BUCK: Tony, tie game, bases loaded, two outs in the bottom of the ninth inning, and your best reliever is due to the plate. Do you pinch hit or let your reliever hit?

TONY LA RUSSA: One of the key parts of that question as you said it is: The bottom of the ninth, which means we're playing at home. One thing you always are aware of, if you're playing at

GAME DECISIONS

home, is you will get that extra three outs to win the game. A lot will depend on how you read your bullpen and how you read your chances to go a couple of extra innings. For example, if you have your best reliever in the game, is he well rested? He might have gone into that game with just one inning to pitch, and he's already pitched it. If he's strong, and you think you can get three outs the next inning from him, it isn't the worst thing in the world to let him go ahead and hit and play the top of the tenth, because he's probably not going to get a base hit. The other factor to consider is the quality of your pinch hitter. Do you have somebody like a Willie McGee on the bench that you have a very good feeling you could take the best reliever out of the game and have a great chance to win? I think what you would put together there is the quality of your pinch hitter, how well rested your bullpen is, and how does your club compare against the other one? In other words, the longer you play, do you have a better or worse chance to win, and then you decide to roll the dice.

JOE BUCK: **Tony, the Cardinals are on the road leading by one in the bottom of the ninth inning. The home team has one out and a good base runner on third. The batter hits a fly ball foul down the right field line. Do you want your outfielder or your infielder to go back and catch the pop up and hope that he can turn and throw the runner out at the plate? Or should he let the ball drop and hope you can get the batter still on the next pitch and win the ball game?**

TONY LA RUSSA: That's a very good question, and it's really a tough one. To me, one thing missing from the question is what the count would be. For example, if the count is 2-0 and the guy hits a pop up, I'd probably catch it and take the tie. If the count is 0-2, I'd probably let it drop. The reasoning is: If you've got 0-2, you're ahead in the count; there's a lot of ways that you might be able to strike out, get a little feeble ground ball, or a pop up the guy at third could not score on. But if the hitter is ahead in the count, then you always have to remember: If this guy gets on base, he becomes the winning run. There's only one thing worse than

GAME DECISIONS

having that tying run score and not winning in the ninth, and that's if you play a little later on and you lose the game anyway. I think the count and how well you feel you can get this hitter out determines whether that ball should be caught or not.

JOE BUCK: Tony, in this specialty era with middle relievers, set-up men and closers, why would a manager ever let a pitcher hit for himself from about the sixth inning on, unless it were a blowout or the pitcher is having one of those special games?

TONY LA RUSSA: The most obvious answer is that you need to be careful with your bullpen, because you can blow out your bullpen. When you think about playing six or seven days a week, and if the last four innings of the game — the last twelve outs — are being put in the hands of your relievers day in and day out, you're going to run through so many relievers. You're going to have them so fatigued or injured before the season is halfway through that you'd suffer for it. What you want to do is monitor the game. When you talk about a starting pitcher having a special game, to me that just means he's pitching effectively. What you always want to do when you get to the second half of the game is: Try to figure out what's the toughest way you can make the other club have to scramble for runs? You start with the pitcher. Is he the guy who would be the toughest for the other side? And if it's the starter, then as long as he's got a chance, at least you know what he's throwing. When you go to the bullpen, you're never positive on how that reliever will come into the game. At least you know the starter. So, to me, you want to preserve your bullpen and go with the starter as long as you can.

GAME DECISIONS

JOE BUCK: Tony, what is the purpose behind the double-switch? And do you ever worry about using it and then getting caught later with your better players already out of the game?

TONY LA RUSSA: Absolutely, you should worry about the double-switch. In fact, the best advice I had coming into the National League was from a good friend, Mr. Leyland. He told me that, in his time in the National League, he's seen more managers try to show how smart they are by double-switching and worked themselves into a hole where they had actually removed their best players. The double-switch is a technique — I think Gene Mauch is one of the guys given credit for developing it — in which you're allowed to bring in a pitcher and substitute him for a player. Where the pitcher's spot probably is coming up the next inning, you have the player hit in that spot. Instead of having the easy out of the pitcher, you have a position player. You almost never want to double-switch with the middle of your lineup, which are your better hitters. What you run into sometimes is, if the pitcher is coming in, then probably the number one consideration is if the pitcher you're bringing in is being figured for one inning or more. If it's more, then you want to consider the double-switch. If the double switch would involve the middle of your lineup, you should figure out something else to do. If the pitcher is coming in for one inning only, then don't worry about it, because you're going to pinch-hit for him anyway.

JOE BUCK: Tony, in a close game, your relief pitcher is cruising but there's a good hitter on deck who hits from the opposite side. If you change pitchers, you gain a platoon advantage but you may lose a little momentum. In situations like this, how much do you rely on statistics and percentages as opposed to your gut feeling about the ability of the pitcher in the current game situation?

TONY LA RUSSA: This is a very difficult question to answer, because there's so many variables here. If you have a relief pitcher who's pitching effectively, I think your natural inclination is to go

GAME DECISIONS

with that pitcher, because of the other rule you learn the hard way all the time. No matter what you think about the reliever you're bringing in, you don't know until he comes in that day what kind of stuff he will have or how sharp he's going to be. If you have a relief pitcher who is pitching effectively, that's something that's a given. Now, with all that said, the match-up is another variable to look at. You have to look at if that match-up is really tough for that relief pitcher who's cruising. In other words, the pitcher who's cruising can get very uncomfortable in a minute if the hitter coming up is a very tough match-up for him. Sometimes you do have some numbers; you may see the guy is very successful against him for his career, and they're not going to pinch hit for him. You may want to make a move. There's a lot of things to put together there, but to me, the key is you're always trying to make it the toughest that you can on the hitter coming to bat.

JOE BUCK: Tony, on what pitch counts are you most likely to call a pitchout?

TONY LA RUSSA: I'm most likely to call a pitchout on the pitch I think is the one they're more likely going to run on. This is the interesting part of the running game because different runners and different managers have different strategies. I remember a manager in the American League who loved to hit-and-run 0-1. He was very sharp, because that's such an unlikely hit-and-run situation, he would never get a pitchout on that particular throw. You finally scouted him, and he did it often enough against you so that you started reading that tendency. To me, what you do is to try to see the other club's tendencies. There's a runner in the National League who likes to run on the second pitch. Whether it's 1-0 or 0-1, this guy, who's a very good base stealer, tends to run, and we've actually pitched out on him a lot in the last couple of years by just going on the fact that he will run on the second pitch. I think the pitchout is something you use when you think the run is likely. You do it sometimes in a hit-and-run situation. I'll tell you when it comes up a lot. It's a little bit risky, but 2-2 is a count where managers like to start the runner. If you pitchout successfully,

GAME DECISIONS

suddenly you've got the guy thrown out. You do have a 3-2 count, but at least you don't have a runner on base. However, if you miss, now you've got 3-2 and the runner's still on first base.

JOE BUCK: Tony, when would you call for a double steal with runners on first and third?

TONY LA RUSSA: A double steal is when you think the catcher is throwing the ball through. The double steal is when the runner on first breaks as the ball gets thrown to second base, then as he stops to avoid the tag, the runner on third heads for home and beats the return throw to the plate. Now, what are the factors there? Obviously, you've got to believe the defense is going to throw the ball through. There are three or four things they can do when you start the runner at first. One thing is a fake. Another is to throw back to the pitcher. Sometimes you can throw to a crashing infielder. So you have to believe the ball is going through. The other thing you look for is how close to the bag your middle infielders are. Who's got second base cover responsibility? Here's a key point: How athletic is he in his movement and how strong and accurate is his arm? There are some infielders in the National League who, if you've got everything going for you — you may have a very good runner at third base or you may have the ball going through — but the guy, somebody like a Rey Ordonez for example, is so quick and has got such a strong, accurate arm, that you want to be careful with the double steal. However, if the other things are in place, it's obviously a great play.

JOE BUCK: Tony, with nobody out and runners at first and third, how do you decide whether to sacrifice the runner to second and have second and third, or to squeeze and try to advance both runners and get a run?

TONY LA RUSSA: There's one play that's a lot more conservative, and in most cases makes more sense. In other words, you've got first and third with nobody out. If you successfully sacrifice a man

GAME DECISIONS

from first to second, now you've got — I'm talking about the pitcher hitting, your leadoff man coming up — you've got second and third with one out, and you've got a very good chance to get a run or both runs. If you squeeze with first and third with nobody out, what are you looking at there? You're really adding to the risk, because a squeeze is a risky play. You can get a pop up, which will equal a double play. You can get a bunt-through — in other words, the pitcher misses the bunt, so he just bunts right through it — you tag the runner coming home. If you have the other runner on second base with the pitcher hitting, there goes your rally. So, it's probably a play that you have to use if you have a perfect circumstance in which the pitcher on the mound is going to be around the plate. You really must have a tremendous amount of confidence that your pitcher at the plate can handle a bat. A guy like Andy Benes is one of the best I've seen since I've been with the Cardinals. He would be a good guy to do it with.

JOE BUCK: Tony, it's the middle innings of the game, and you're trailing by one run. There's one out. The bases are loaded, and your pitcher's at bat. What factors go into your decision to pinch-hit for him or let that pitcher hit?

TONY LA RUSSA: The factors that I would pay the most attention to are the fact that it's the middle innings, and it's a one run game. That tells you it's a close ballgame, and there's still quite a bit of game to play. What you would look at is whether the one run game is 8-7, 7-6. So, in other words, you would look at whether your pitcher has been struggling. If he's pitching well, which is what I would assume here, there's still some innings to be played. I would let him stay in the ballgame, especially if he had a chance to swing the bat decently. You might even consider a squeeze, even though it's bases loaded. I think the big factor is: You want to stop the other club first, then you think about scoring runs. When you have several innings to play, and if your pitcher on the mound has still got stuff to get the other side out, you're going to be tempted to leave him in the game. Any time you make a move to bring in a pitcher, you're never sure what the reliever is going to bring in.

GAME DECISIONS

You're watching the guy who is on the mound, so you see exactly how sharp and how strong he is, but the reliever, no matter how good he is that day, may be different than what you expect. I would look at how the pitcher is, what the score is, how much time is left, and whether he can swing the bat. I would tend to let him stay in the ballgame if he's still pitching well.

JOE BUCK: **Tony, how do you decide whether to use your best pinch-hitter in the middle innings of the game or hold him and use him later in the ballgame?**

TONY LA RUSSA: The key is to try to anticipate the real inning of decision. In most games, you play 9 innings, so that's 27 outs for both clubs. However, not every out is the same. You're going to have some crucial situations where, if you're trying to get the out, making it gets you the win. If you're trying to get a hit in that situation, if you get it you win. Your pinch-hitter, your best pinch-hitter, is one of the weapons you go into a game looking to use at the right time. Normally, you would hold that guy for later in the game, because no matter what you do in the middle part of the game, you still have more game to play, and if he does something well, they might overcome it. You would need him later on. The closer that you can get a key player to perform his key thing at the end, in which less of the game is left, the better chance you have to win. Usually, you try to save your best guy for the key situation late in the game. However, you may read a game. It's one of those momentum things, and perhaps you're behind and all of a sudden the bases are loaded, and it's the middle of the game. So you have a chance to bring in your guy, and he can turn the tide in your favor. There are times where it is important to use that best pinch-hitter early, but I would say that the general rule is you would hold him until later.

GAME DECISIONS

JOE BUCK: Tony, your ball club's down by two in the eighth, and you've got runners at the corners on first and third with nobody out, and your number eight hitter's coming up. What do you do in that situation?

TONY LA RUSSA: I think what you're supposing there is that your eighth-place hitter is not a productive offensive player. Immediately you would think to hit for him, because you're talking about late in the game and being down by two runs, and there is that tying run on first base with nobody out. That's a great run-scoring and crooked-number inning, so I would pick the best runner I had in that situation and send him up for the eighth place hitter. What I would not do is bunt the eighth-place hitter to get the runner to second. That's something you might want to do with the pitcher if you didn't want to remove the pitcher. You wouldn't want to trade an out in that situation when you've only got six left. The other thing you can do, which is a good play if the pitcher's around the plate and if your hitter can handle the bat, is play a hit-and-run. That would get the runner home from third and advance the runner to second. You may trade an out, but it's more of an aggressive play, because if the guy happens to get a ground ball to go through the infield, then you're looking at first and third, nobody out with the tying run at third base. My options would be: pinch-hit, or if not at least do something aggressive like a hit-and-run.

JOE BUCK: Tony, your ball club's ahead by a couple of runs in the eighth inning. The other team has runners at the corners at first and third with nobody out and their number eight hitter coming up. What do you do to try to keep the lead?

TONY LA RUSSA: This is the kind of question that has all kinds of ways to go depending on the situation, because the situation can really change. For example, what type of hitter is the eighth-place hitter? How good a runner do you have on first base? What if the guy on first base runs really well? You want to be able to have somebody on the mound who can defend the running game. I think an important point you're always getting to late in the game

GAME DECISIONS

is: You want to try to make it as tough to score as possible for the other side. That's why you see some of these multiple changes of relievers, because one reliever might be tough against one hitter, but the next hitter comes up and he's not as tough against him, so you bring somebody else in. That's where that theory started, and that's why you see so much of it. However, if you're thinking in that situation, the run at third probably is going to score and you're looking at a one-run lead, then your big consideration is how to keep the guy at first from scoring. You want to be able to look at who's on the mound and who's in the bullpen, and one key is: You want to have your bullpen active and ready in case the other side makes a pinch-hitting move, so you can be ready to counter it.

JOE BUCK: Tony, who typically calls pitchouts, and what factors go into making that sort of a decision?

TONY LA RUSSA: It depends on the ball club. The manager has the responsibility, but sometimes, like other pieces of the club, he delegates it to other people. On our ball club, I was taught to handle as much of that stuff as you can because it's your butt on the line, and it's your way to earn some respect from your team if you do it well. Some managers have a bench coach who they think has a real feel for it, and that responsibility will go to that bench coach. I think it's probably 50-50 in the big leagues between the managers and the bench coaches, and even when you have a bench coach, the manager can say in this particular case, "Right now, let's call one." What are the factors? I think you really try to read the tendency of the other club. Some managers are more aggressive in the running game and the hit-and-run game. You want to look at who the base runner is, and you want to look at the game situation, such as the outs. A lot of the situations just cry out at you that the other side really wants to do something to push the guy on first base. One way you counter is with a pitchout. There are some counts that are prime running counts, and you pitchout then. But you've always got to run the risk of getting that count against your pitcher if you're wrong.

GAME DECISIONS

JOE BUCK: Tony, in a tight game, what goes into your decision as a ball club whether to give up the run in hopes for an inning-ending double play?

TONY LA RUSSA: Sometimes that decision is just made for you. If the guy at the plate runs very fast, and there's no chance to make that double play unless he hits a hot smash one-hopper right at somebody, then you're probably going to have to get the run at the plate and avoid the double play. However, most of the time you have considerations, such as winning on the road versus winning at home. If you're playing at home, and you have the lead — for example, it's first and third and that run at home ties — you still will bat in the bottom of the inning. You'll always get your last chance to bat, so you may lay back and play for the double play. If you miss the double play, the tying run scores. If you're on the road, you may want to take your chance and come in to cut the run off at the plate, because the longer you play on the road, usually the advantage is to the home team. You would change that if you think you're the stronger club and have the stronger bullpen, which is probably the key. You still might want to play back for the double play and go ahead and take the tie, because you figure you're better than they are. Then, the longer you play the better chance you have to win. It really comes down to an analysis of what's your best chance to win and how good you think you are versus them.

JOE BUCK: Tony, when your starter is struggling early in a ballgame, how do you decide how long to let him go before you go to your bullpen?

TONY LA RUSSA: This is probably one of the toughest situations for a manager because he's struggling. For example, he gives up four or five runs in the first couple of innings, and you've got a lot of factors that are working against you — besides the fans being unhappy. One of the factors is: The more runs he gives up, the harder it is for you to come back and win the game. However, you're also weighing that versus the fact that, as soon as you relieve him, your bullpen is going to have more of the game to

GAME DECISIONS

pitch. On some days, that's a real burden. If you've been working your bullpen a lot, you may not have six or seven innings in that pen without taking a chance of hurting somebody. So, I think you look at the starter. Is he the kind of guy who, if you can get him through, he'll find a routine and start clicking along and give you a chance to win? Is he a guy who, if he doesn't get it going good early, has been known to blow up and never have another chance? Then you look at your bullpen. Can we pitch the rest of this game with our relievers and have a chance to win? You put that all together, and it's a very difficult call.

JOE BUCK: Tony, your closer is well rested, but he hasn't had a lot of success against the team you're playing that night. Do you use him to close that game or do you give someone else a shot?

TONY LA RUSSA: Well, if he's your closer, and he's a legitimate closer who is well rested, then the worst thing you can do is not give him the opportunity to close the game. What you don't want to do with any player — especially with the closer who has to work with a deep sense of confidence and the sense of feeling confident among his teammates, manager and coaches — is to start calling on somebody else in these situations. If you look at the club that he struggles against, there are probably players that hit him hard and other ones that he gets out. You might want to try to straddle the fence a little bit on by looking at who's going to come up in that ninth inning. An easy one would be: If you see the leadoff hitter is a left-hand hitter who really kills him, then maybe you'll want to bring in your left-hand reliever against that left-handed hitter and then you go to the right-handed closer. My answer is: I would be very conscious of having that confidence in him, but I would also try to win the game. Maybe there's a way you can split some hairs and do both. But in no case would I want him to think that I don't think he can get this club out this night, because that would transfer over in a bad way for other games.

GAME DECISIONS

JOE BUCK: Tony, your closer has worked several nights in a row, but you're playing a team that he's worked very well against in his past. Do you rest him, or do you use him again to close? In other words, how do you fight the urge to overwork your closer?

TONY LA RUSSA: I think one of the answers would definitely depend on what time of the year it is. If you're getting near the end of the season, you may not have the luxury of resting him. If you need the game badly, you may have to push him — especially against the club he's really dominated, because they know it and he knows it and it would be a different type of save. Normally, if he's worked several nights in a row, you're always remembering that, sometimes, you have to risk losing a game rather than lose a pitcher or a player. I think normally you would not send him out there. You would try to find a different way to win that game, by giving the opportunity to somebody else, and it happens. You can make a hero of one of your other relievers, or maybe a starter who's in between starts can come out there and be used in the bullpen that day. That will help your ball club, because other guys contributing to the win gives you a feeling of depth and all that stuff. The key thing you're thinking about is: If I break my closer, I'm going to lose several games down the road. In any case, I'd rather lose one game than to lose one of the key guys on your club.

JOE BUCK: Tony, do you ever steal on a strange count or just do something that's totally opposite "the book" just to cross up the other side?

TONY LA RUSSA: I think the answer is yes, but the more important issue is why? You can do things that are really a surprise, but they're stupid. All you serve there is to hurt your club's chance to win. Just to give you a screwy example: A man is on third, and you have McGwire squeeze. Now, there's no way the book says that, and there's no way the other team is looking for it,

GAME DECISIONS

but that's just a dumb play. I think the key is: There are some times the way the game is going, especially if it's not going your way — and I think that's really the answer, if the game is not going your way — staying by the book just means you're going to lose by the book. You may want to do something that's very different because it might jolt your side and the other side and give you some momentum. Baseball is amazing this way. If you change the momentum in your direction, you can be surprised sometimes at how many runs you can get on the board before they can stop the momentum against you. I would only use that crazy play when things are not looking very good.

JOE BUCK: **Tony, your starting pitcher's going along pretty well, and then about the seventh inning he gets pulled for a relief pitcher. Why not just let him pitch?**

TONY LA RUSSA: That's one of those questions that I think come up during a game. Fans are watching, and they see a pitcher, just like Joe explained, who is going along pretty well, and then somebody else comes out there. There are several things that could have happened. One, he might have come in and complained about some physical problem, in which case the decision is made for you. However, more often than not, you're watching very closely and you see his stuff start to change. There's an old rule that a guy can only pitch out of so many jams before the tank is void of any gas, so you look at how difficult the game's been on him. It's true that, normally, as you get into the last part of the game and you want to go to your bullpen, if you can anticipate the trouble, you have a better chance to avoid it if you know the pitcher is starting to fatigue. Another hit or two, you let him create the trouble, and then ask your reliever to end it. What you do a lot is read these signs and see the pitcher's done or just about to be done, so you give the bullpen a little margin of error when they come in to save the game.

GAME DECISIONS

JOE BUCK: Tony, bottom of the ninth inning, runners on first and third, you're down by two runs with two outs. Should the runner on first try to steal second to get into scoring position?

TONY LA RUSSA: It depends, because you have to look at a lot of different situations. For one, who's the hitter at bat? If it's your most dangerous hitter, all you're doing by stealing the base is opening that base and probably taking the bat out of his hands. They'll either walk him intentionally, even though he's the go-ahead run, or they'll pitch him so tough he won't get anything good to hit. This is because a base hit will keep it going, and you'll open up the hole for him if the runner stays on there. I think the best answer is — assuming that he's not your most dangerous hitter, which isn't going to happen most of the time — whether the stolen base is available. One thing is definite: If you get to second base, a base hit ties the game. A base hit, if you stay at first, is going to make you have to get another hit, so you need to look at if the stolen base is available. You look at all the normal stuff: How quick is the guy to the plate? How well does the guy throw? And how quick is your runner? If those things are going for you, definitely take the base, because one base hit ties the game instead of getting you one run closer.

JOE BUCK: Tony, when you are facing a good base stealer, how do you decide when to pitchout?

TONY LA RUSSA: There are several keys. Obviously, the speed of the runner is a key, but you also look for situations in the game. Sometimes the other side is really going to push, and other times they're going to be more conservative. However, some of the keys are: The count — there are some running counts. It could be that, if you were talking about stealing a base, a base stealer would look for a breaking ball count, because they don't want to run on a fastball. If you're looking for just a running situation where you think the guy may be playing hit-and-run, usually you do that in the opposite, when the count is in the hitter's favor, such as 1-0, 2-1, 2-0. As far as a good base stealer, you look for counts and you

GAME DECISIONS

look for situations. However, the other things you really try, and that's why you see some of these delays in the game, are when the pitchers are holding the ball and stepping off or throwing over, a base stealer will many times tip off whether he's running or not by the way he takes his stance. They get a little lazy if they're not running. They kind of settle in. Then all of a sudden, when they're going to try to run that pitch, you'll see them get a little more antsy or maybe their body will be a little more coiled, so you look for the tip-offs, such as they may extend their leads. Some guys even reduce their lead when they're going to run. So any of those keys can cause a pitchout.

JOE BUCK: **Tony, how do you determine when you can use a relief pitcher on consecutive days?**

TONY LA RUSSA: The factors you look at are: Number one, the pitcher himself. How resilient is his arm? Guys differ. In fact, the very valuable relievers are the ones who have the so-called "rubber arms" that can throw a lot. That's why it's so important to monitor pitches. You've gone through spring training, so you know a certain stamina level for all of your pitchers whether they're relievers or starters. For example, on Tuesday a guy like a Mike Timlin could probably give you 30 pitches if he's rested. On Tuesday, if he gave you 10 or 12, you know easily that he'll be available the next day. I think you monitor pitches, and you get to learn the type of pitcher he is. Can he bounce back the next day? I'll tell you one of the most important keys — and this is something you stress to players because of their nature to try to be heroes — is for them to tell you the truth. You know a guy may have thrown 10 pitches that may have been very awkward for him, and he may be a little extra stiff or sore, but it looks like he should be able to go. He'll tell you he's available, but really and truly he shouldn't go because he's not feeling right. He needs to tell you the truth. That's the one thing we really preach to our relievers: If they're not available, tell us. It's a long season, but you put those things together and you figure out whether you can repeat them.

GAME DECISIONS

JOE BUCK: Tony, with a man on third and less than two outs, when would you consider intentionally walking a batter to set up a double play situation?

TONY LA RUSSA: I think common sense has to rule here. If the guy at the plate is more dangerous than the guy coming up, then obviously you may want to choose that. When you've got to be careful is, every time you put a base runner on base in one of these run-scoring situations, you're adding to the chance the inning could get away from you. The classic time would be: Open base and the guy on deck is not as good a hitter as the guy at the plate, and the guy on deck does not have the kind of speed that you would worry whether he could beat a double play if he does hit a ground ball. However, sometimes the opposite happens. You see the open base, but with the guy at bat, if we go against this guy aggressively and we try to make tough pitches, we can get this guy to hit a weak pop up or maybe strike him out. Or, at the same time, the guy on deck is somebody that if he hits a ground ball side to side to an infielder, we won't turn two, so you've defeated the purpose of adding a base runner and opening up the risk of a bigger inning. So to me, it's if you really have a chance to retire that guy if he doesn't run well enough to beat the double play.

JOE BUCK: Tony, when selecting a pinch-hitter, do you look more at lefty-righty match-ups or that individual's record against the pitcher who's on the mound?

TONY LA RUSSA: Mostly what you look at is to evaluate the strength of the pitcher or his weakness, and you try to evaluate the hitters you have on the bench and how they match up. Usually, you don't have a lot of numbers to go with. It's much easier to make a decision for a starting pitcher because you may have 30,40,20 at bats. For a reliever, you know, you may have like a one for four, so what does that tell you? It's much more important if you have a righthand sinkerballer, then you look for a down hitter, or if you have a high-ball hitter, then you don't try to match him up with a sinkerballer. If you've got a guy who chases the ball up, don't use

GAME DECISIONS

him if you can help it against a pitcher that throws a lot of fastballs up in the zone. Some guys have a slow bat, so maybe they're better breaking ball hitters. If you have a reliever come in against you who really features forkballs and sliders and change-ups, you don't want somebody who's got the quickest bat. So, you put all of those things together. I think lefty-righty is a factor, because some right-handers are very nasty against right-hand hitters, but I don't think you go crazy with lefty-righty. I think it's more with matching the type of pitching against the type of hitting that you have.

JOE BUCK: Tony, are bench players essentially assigned to certain roles they pretty much know about ahead of time?

TONY LA RUSSA: I think we talk about building the bench, and on your bench you may have guys that are your fourth outfielder — the guy that may be on the club more to play when one of your regular outfielders doesn't go that day. Or you have your extra infielder who may play as a regular, and you also may have this specialist on your bench. For example, you have a couple of guys you really think are your best pinch-hitters that day. Then what you want to try to do is save them for that point in the game where the toughest at bat is needed from your bench. If you had a sixth-inning, two-out situation, and you're pinch-hitting for your pitcher with nobody on base, then you're not going to waste your best hitter there. You're going to try to save him for later in the game. You also really need to look at the other side's bullpen and try to figure out whom you are likely to see late in the game and who's your best match up. For example, if you have a tough left-hander out there, and if Polanco on our club is not playing, he's the best right-hand pinch-hitter we have. If, on this club right now, you've got a tough right-hander, then right now Larry Sutton has got the best chance to have a good at bat. You don't want to waste those guys early, and they know that you save them for later since the other guys are used earlier in the games.

GAME DECISIONS

JOE BUCK: Tony, with the game on the line and a slumping star at bat, how do you decide whether to pinch-hit for that star or let the big guy bat?

TONY LA RUSSA: What game is on the line? I'm not being facetious when I say or ask that. Is it a game toward the end of the season where you're running out of games, and if you're in first place or by winning the game you've got a better chance to win first place? Or if you're behind, you can't afford to mug another game. As those stakes change, then I think you have to be more concerned with that game versus the whole season. If it happens in the first couple of months, and you're trying to get your big stars going, you don't want to make him think you don't have confidence in him. There are a lot of times you manage for the season, and not for that particular game or that series. So I really think it depends on what part of the season, because ultimately there's a comfort factor as a manager. If I go into a ballgame, and every decision I make is geared to what's the best way to win this game for our team, then you can face anyone, no matter how much they disagree with you. However, if you start messing around with who the guy is and whether I'm afraid to make a decision, you'll end up getting burned. So, as long as I think it's going to help us win now or later, I'm okay with it.

JOE BUCK: Tony, relievers often come in and pitch an effective inning, and then they're replaced. What are the risks and benefits of using guys one inning at a time?

TONY LA RUSSA: This is a terrific question, in my opinion, because I think this is one that fans who are watching the game closely really get into, and it happens a lot. And why do they get into it? Because a pitcher comes in there and, for example, he gets 1, 2, 3, and then another pitcher comes out there the next inning, so the fans are scratching their heads and saying, "Now, wait a minute. Why did they do that? I wouldn't have done it that way." So, what are the reasons that you would do it? One reason is that you learn some guys are not good sitting on the bench and waiting

GAME DECISIONS

for the next inning to start. I'm telling you the truth about this. Relievers get ready in the bullpen, then they come in — they're all maxed out, they go 1, 2, 3. But when they sit, they are not able to play catch and get ready, so it disrupts their routine. You'll see guys pacing. You'll see guys go crazy on that, and when they go back out there, they've got no clue. I mean, it's not the same pitcher. So, you've got a tendency not to want to send that guy out for longer than the one inning. Other times, it may be the only thing you have for that guy on that day is one inning. For a guy like Steve Kline on our club right now, if this guy pitches more than one inning too many times, he's not going to be available enough times in games that we have a chance to win. So you have to be careful with that, too.

JOE BUCK: Tony, what factors go into deciding when to hold against a runner at first base and when not to hold against them?

TONY LA RUSSA: The biggest thing is: Who's the hitter at the plate? The best example of that is the left-handed pull hitter, because if you're holding the runner at first and you've got the second baseman in his normal position, that's a huge hole for that left-handed pull hitter to hit a ground ball into right field. If you think about a ground ball to right field, the runner's going to go to third base and, depending on the outs, you're looking at a tough run-scoring situation against you. When you're holding that runner on, you're opening a hole, but if you play behind that runner, you take that hole away and the guy at first base probably is going to run to second. So what you try to look at is how about the runner at first who doesn't have any speed. Then you can play behind him and not worry about the stolen base. Sometimes what we try to do is play right behind the guy, and not let him get much of a lead, thus trying to discourage him from stealing. I think the most important thing is the score. Does the runner at first having a chance to score hurt you more than the guy at bat? If you've got a two-run lead, then go ahead and play behind him late in the game, because what you need there is outs. You're not worried so

GAME DECISIONS

much about the guy at first scoring, since you just don't want the guy at the plate to get on base. So it depends on the type of hitter and the score.

JOE BUCK: **Tony, on your ball club, whose decision is it to steal a base? Is it the players, the coaches, or does the manager give the signs from the bench every time?**

TONY LA RUSSA: The way we go on this club, is it would be either the player or the manager. In some places, the manager assigns the base running to a coach, to a bench coach for example, and he runs it. However, I don't think most managers do that. What you do is try to decide if the player has good judgment as far as when to run, and he can get the green light. And for those guys, occasionally when the game dictates, you may give them a "don't run" sign or a red light. But any other time, they have the decision to go. There are some guys you don't feel have the same type of good judgment, and good judgment to me is a high-percentage stealer. If you're going to steal, then you had better steal 10 out of 12 for the season. If you're going to steal 30, then it had better be 30 out of 40. For the guys you feel do not have that same kind of judgment, then the manager has to flash the signs. What you're looking for there is, if the count is against the hitter, then maybe you want to go ahead and try to risk stealing a base. If you get thrown out, your hitter starts fresh the next inning. A real common strategy I see a lot of guys do is trying to push a stolen base with two outs. Rather than trying to make the third out at second base, they do something aggressively and start fresh with a hitter the next inning, rather than just go and let the hitter make an out with nothing risked there.

OFFENSE

JOE BUCK: Tony, everybody talks about getting the platoon advantage in terms of batting average, matching your left-handed hitter against a right-handed pitcher and vice versa. How important is that to you? And at times does that get overblown a bit?

TONY LA RUSSA: Yes, here again I think it's people look at a certain formula for managing and for dictating match-ups, who don't look at the meat of what's really happening. You have to really evaluate your hitter. It's not just numbers. A right-handed hitter will not always hit a left-handed pitcher better and vice versa. Some right-handed hitters are better against right-handed pitchers. Some left-handed hitters are very good hanging in there against left-handed pitchers. I think what you want to look for is really how much of a problem do you have. If you have a guy who struggles against one side, then as part of putting your club together, you look for that complement. You look for the guy to give you that edge against the other side's pitcher. However, just as a matter of routine, to always think the platoon will bring you an advantage is a big mistake. Most good hitters hit against everybody. Most guys that struggle do so for a reason. If the reason is that he sees the ball very well from one side but can't see it from the other, that's the time you use a platoon, and that's the only time.

JOE BUCK: Okay Tony La Russa, here's today's question. In general, it is more difficult for a left-handed batter to contend with a left-handed pitcher than for a right-handed batter to deal with a right-handed pitcher. Now, if you can answer this question, I think you're the best. This is a tough question to answer.

TONY LA RUSSA: Now why is that?

OFFENSE

JOE BUCK: Why is that? Who knows why?

TONY LA RUSSA: I think there is a good reason. I'm going to give you the reason that was explained to me, and it makes a lot of sense. There are so many more right-handed pitchers than there are left-handed pitchers that a right-handed hitter has to survive. As he grows up, whether it's Little League, American Legion, high school ball, or college ball, over and over he has to deal with a right-handed pitcher to be successful. You never get to the big leagues unless, as a right-handed hitter, you have hit right-handed pitchers. If you look at how few left-handed pitchers there really are coming up through and including the big leagues, there are much more right-handed pitchers than left-handed pitchers. The left-handed hitter doesn't get as much exposure and doesn't really learn to make the adjustments that you need to make. I think it's a truism that when you get to the big leagues, guys like Lankford and Mabry who hit left-handers so well are so unique that it's a big advantage. The very good left-handed hitters handle all pitching. I think the biggest explanation where you see a definite difference in why platooning makes sense is: Left-handed hitters just do not have enough experience against left-handed pitchers, and by the time you get to the big leagues that's not the time to start giving them that experience.

JOE BUCK: Okay Tony La Russa, here's today's question. The Cardinals are tied in extra innings and have slow runners on first and second base with nobody out. Do you have the next hitter bunt or do you let him swing away?

TONY LA RUSSA: That's one of those situations where the book says you bunt, but the idea is; Whatever play you put on, you have to feel like you have a chance to succeed. With a force play retiring the runner advancing to third, it's a very difficult bunt to lay down. You have the other team who is usually defending the bunt very aggressively, so what you try to do is run for the slow runner at second base. If you can make that move, that obviously helps your chances. If you can't, and

OFFENSE

you're really stuck with slow runners, I've found it helps to keep the defense guessing. You may start out having the hitter swing and that keeps the defense a little more honest — they'll play back a little bit. For the next pitch, you can switch to a bunt. Another good option, especially if you have a hitter who puts the ball in play, is to play hit-and-run, start your runners, and have the hitter attempt to put the ball in play on the ground.

JOE BUCK: Okay Tony, here's today's question. A lot of hitters don't like facing a knuckleball pitcher. Do most hitters have a certain pitch that they don't like to hit?

TONY LA RUSSA: I think so, because while you have some hitters who feel they can hit everything all the time, most hitters will tell you there's some pitch they know is very difficult for them. A knuckleball is a great example. A lot of players don't like to hit it because it's just so wacky, and you have to adjust your mechanics and your thinking. Also, it tends to affect you the day before you face him and the day after you face him and all that stuff. Some players who are low-ball hitters don't like to face a high fastball power pitcher. Some guys who are better fastball hitters than breaking ball hitters don't like to see the pitcher with very good breaking stuff. Some hitters look like they're just as weird as they can be if anybody throws a changeup. They're always just flailing at it, so there's a pitch that troubles every hitter. If you have a pitcher who has all four of them, that guy should be a very good pitcher.

JOE BUCK: Okay Tony, here is today's question. Can certain pitchers put an entire team in a slump?

TONY LA RUSSA: I think it's possible you can pick up a problem facing a type of pitcher. I think the most obvious one for years in the American League was going against Charlie Hough. He would drive you nuts. The next day or two, it just didn't look like you had the same kind of swing as before you faced him. I think someone

OFFENSE

who is really a great off-speed type of pitcher and who is really soft can really mess with your timing so badly that it's tough to get back in a groove. I've also seen someone who is very overpowering and it embarrasses you, so the next day there is a carryover and your club is not as confident. So, it is possible for a very outstanding pitcher to have an effect on the day he beats you and for it to carry over for 2 or 3 games. For me, the challenge is when you see something like that happen, you have to be able to turn the page and wipe that bad game out of your mind.

JOE BUCK: Okay Tony La Russa, here's today's question. Why do even accomplished big league hitters have a difficult time with hitting the off-speed pitch?

TONY LA RUSSA: I think it really depends, because when you say a big league hitter is going to have trouble hitting it, then it has to be a couple of things. Number one, it has to be a quality breaking pitch, off-speed pitch, and it has to be at a quality location. If you think about hitting and pitching, what a pitcher tries to mess with, as far as a hitter, is his balance and his timing. Balance is usually affected by moving the ball in and out where the guy is either leaning out over the plate or having to back off it. Timing, though, is affected by velocity. You put a little on, and you take a little off. So the off-speed pitch can be very effective if it's thrown to a location that is not up in the strike zone, where even though you may have a guy's timing messed up, it's up enough to where the guy could really center-hit it for distance. You've got to get the off-speed pitch down and out of the happy zone. Finally, the off-speed pitch has to have enough of a difference in velocity from his other pitches to where you really fool the hitter, as far as timing.

OFFENSE

JOE BUCK: We often see players bunt to get a runner from first to second. If the bunt is such a good percentage play to advance a runner, then why isn't it more commonly used to get a runner from third to home, such as with a squeeze play?

TONY LA RUSSA: That's a good question. There's a lot in this question, such as: Is the bunt that good of a percentage play? I think you have to be very careful when you remember there are only 27 outs in a game. Every time you give up one of them by virtue of a bunt, you really have to believe that you have a better chance to score if the runner gets to second base and you get the out. I've said this many times — strategy is just a person's opinion, and opinions differ. That's one of the beauties of baseball. You can watch the game and you can say, "I would have squeezed; he didn't." I think you have to guard your bunts. Usually, in the National League with a pitcher at bat, it's a safe play or it's a good play to use the out to advance the runner. I like the hit-and-run, because that's a more aggressive play. As far as the squeeze, if you look at it, it's difficult to put on a squeeze because the players who are most likely to squeeze are the ones the opposition is looking for, such as the pitcher or the hitter who doesn't swing the bat very well. Whenever the defense is not looking for it, it's with hitters like a Lankford or a Gant or a Jordan who you are not going to squeeze with. The element of surprise is almost never there with a squeeze, and it's always a guessing game as to when or if they'll pitchout. Usually that means the count is in your favor. A bunt is just a careful play for any manager.

JOE BUCK: Okay Tony La Russa, here is today's question. Is it possible to compromise the effectiveness of the squeeze play by overusing it?

TONY LA RUSSA: Absolutely. The most obvious is if you take the squeeze play and you use it with a hitter who is likely to get the runner in. If you let him swing, what you're doing is sending a message to him saying you don't think he can drive the run home so we're going to take the bat out of your hands and

OFFENSE

bunt. So I think the squeeze play could be overused by a confidence factor that you don't show in your hitters. Also, if you're using it a lot, the other side is paying attention, and it's a play that can be defended. There are ways to defend a squeeze play such as a pitchout or throwing the ball up where you get a pop up and a double play or a bunt-through. It just really diffuses the inning. I think the squeeze play is definitely a weapon. I think it's something you try to put on when the other side is likely to throw a strike. You try not to do it when the bases are loaded so you have the force play at the plate. It's something I think you use occasionally, but you can definitely overuse it.

JOE BUCK: Okay Tony, here's today's question. The sacrifice bunt advances the runner but costs you an out, and you only get 27 of them in a game. What situations make that a worthwhile trade off?

TONY LA RUSSA: It is one of those age-old controversies that you can have in baseball. It's one of the reasons it is so great for fans. What is strategy but just opinion? You're getting the manager's opinion because you can see the result — what he decides is the best move for that particular situation. As a fan you can say, "That is crazy. I would never give up one of my treasured 27 outs with a bunt." The one thing to remember, and I use this a lot, is most hitters are better hitters with a runner at second base than they are with a runner at first. With a runner at first, there is a tendency to want to do something a little bigger — I am going to hit the ball in the gap; I am going to get an extra-base hit. If you get a runner at second base and that same hitter knows that if he just stings the ball, makes hard contact, a lousy single scores the run. I think there are times when giving up one of your outs just to advance the runner to a scoring position is a very good move, especially in a low-scoring game where runs are hard to come by.

OFFENSE

JOE BUCK: Okay Tony, here's today's question. Should a player continue to switch-hit even when there's a great disparity between his left-handed average and his right-handed average?

TONY LA RUSSA: You need to use some judgment on this one. I think there are a couple of points to make at the beginning. Number one, being a switch-hitter is a tremendous advantage. Personally, I think a lot of managers agree with this. They love switch-hitters. I love switch-hitters. They do so much for your ball club, and they create so many problems for the other side. Being a switch-hitter is not only good for the manager and the club, it's really good for your career because you will always have an edge as far as playing time. So the question then becomes, are you a legitimate switch-hitter? Can both sides be nearly the same? You may have a dominant side, which is all right, but the other side can't be so drastically different that it's a waste or just an out every time up there. You have to make a judgment. I think if you're early on in your learning, you can expect to have some problems. If you do it for a lot of years and you finally have gotten to where you're hitting .100 one way and .300 the other way, then you're probably going to have to give it up.

JOE BUCK: Are there perfect hit-and-run situations, and is there ever a time when you would definitely not want to use the hit-and-run?

TONY LA RUSSA: I think if I tried to describe the perfect hit-and-run, one way to look at it is when you wouldn't want to do it is when one of these factors is missing. The perfect hit-and-run is a pitcher against you who is around the plate with less than strikeout stuff. For example, it's a sinkerball pitcher, because another part of the perfect situation is a ball thrown in the strike zone, usually from mid-thigh down. When that ball's put into play, it will be on the ground. If you play hit-and-run, and the guy hits the ball in the air, you're not going to get the base advance. This type of pitcher — a sinkerball — is the best. The best type of hitter is a player who

OFFENSE

really handles the bat, is short in his stroke, and is sure to makes contact somewhere. Finally, the base runner must be somebody who is quick enough that, in case the pitcher makes just a terrible pitch the hitter can't swing at it — it's not anywhere near the plate — the runner can successfully steal second. If you look at those factors, you still might hit-and-run with a pitcher who is not a sinkerball pitcher. Or, you might still hit-and-run with a runner at first who is not a great runner, or a hitter who is not the best bat handler that you have. Usually it comes down to: You may want to do something offensively like the hit-and-run if you are really struggling to score runs.

JOE BUCK: Tony, here is today's question. How exactly does the hit-and-run play work, and in what situation do you like to use it?

TONY LA RUSSA: I think it is one of the more interesting plays that an offense can have. You always have this dilemma of bunting, which costs you an out and advances the base, versus letting the guy swing, which keeps your outs intact but you may never get anything going because runners are never moving off first base. An in-between play which is aggressive is the hit-and-run. When the runner is certain the pitcher is delivering the ball to the plate, he takes off for second base. He glances over his shoulder back towards the plate at about the third step because he wants to see what the hitter is doing. For example, if he pops the ball up, the runner stops and goes back to the base. It's different from a steal where the guy is just going dead set for second base and never looks. The hitter is instructed he has to swing at the ball. His idea is to put the ball on the ground hard anywhere. You don't try to nudge it in the opposite direction. You just try to hit the ball as hard as you can on the ground. I think it is one of those plays you use instead of a bunt at times because it is more aggressive. It's a play you use sometimes when you've got a lead of a run or two. If that play works: Think about it, if you use it with less than 2 outs, it means first and third. You can break open an inning and a ball game by executing it properly. It's an aggressive play. It's usually something you do with a decent runner and a hitter who has some bat control.

OFFENSE

JOE BUCK: Let's say you have a hitter who strikes out a lot. Is strike zone judgment something you can teach, and if so how do you go about doing that?

TONY LA RUSSA: Normally, when you have a hitter who has a strikeout problem, it's the type of stroke he has rather than his judgment of the strike zone. Obviously, if he's one of the classic Bible hitters — you know, "Thou shall not pass!" — that's not going to be too effective. The other club is going to notice this guy swings at everything, and they are just not going to throw a ball over the plate to him. But that's something you can point out to him. It's not that tough. "Look, in the last 50 at bats you've taken, you've only swung at 10 balls in the strike zone. The other 100 have been out." You can point that out to him. I think the biggest bonanza or the biggest area to improve is the stroke. That's where two-strike hitting can really improve and prevent strikeouts, or cut down strikeouts, and that's where we teach him how to be a good two-strike hitter. There are four or five fundamentals all good two-strike hitters use. If a hitter religiously works on doing these things, he will put the ball in play with two strikes, especially when you have good legs. For example, we want Royce and Delino this year to cut their strikeouts down. With their legs, if they just tap the ball into play, they'll increase the number of times they get on base and certainly their strikeouts will go down.

JOE BUCK: So what should a hitter do differently when he has two strikes?

TONY LA RUSSA: Joe, I appreciate that you're still asking this expert, because this manager last year in '97 was not very much of an expert with our club. We struck out way too much. It was maddening and very frustrating, but we're bound and determined to do better this year, because two-strike hitting is a fundamental that you can improve. The first key is for the hitter to understand the importance of putting the ball in play. All of your really good hitters, all the guys who hit for a high average and understand

OFFENSE

what winning offensive play requires, do something different with two strikes. You get down in the count with two strikes, so it's much more important to put the ball in play than to just take a big swing. What are the keys? Most guys will tell you that you should get a little wider in your stance to cut down your stride, and think more compact in your stroke. You don't try to reach for that extra big loop or big arc — that allows you to see the ball a little longer and not commit quite as quickly. Most everybody will tell you that one of the keys is to look middle away and try to hit the ball hard to the middle. If you think about those keys, such as the middle away, hard to the middle, with a shorter stroke, and with less stride, then you will put the ball in play, you will have better timing, and you will be surprised at how hard and far you hit the ball.

JOE BUCK: Before the start of a series, what types of things do you tell your hitters about the other team pitchers?

TONY LA RUSSA: What they don't want to hear is: This pitcher throws fastballs, curve balls, a slider, and change ups. They don't want to hear that because it's just too standard, and it's really not helpful. What they want to hear is: What type of movement does he have with his fastball. Is it a fastball that is up in the strike zone or down? Does it have a little inside run to it or did he cut it across the other side, the first base side of the plate if he's a right-hander? What type of breaking ball does he feature? Very rarely do you have a pitcher that has two equally effective breaking balls. He usually has one that he will go to in a pinch. And then, what is his really soft pitch? Is it a change up? Is it a forkball? When does he use it, and how often? Then they want to learn about his style. Is he the kind of pitcher who, with nobody on base, he'll really come after you with fastballs early? What are his out pitches, especially with men on base? They want to know how he gets ahead of counts. Pitchers will develop patterns. They will try to get strike one with something, and they like to finish you off with something else. If you can give hitters that information, it helps their preparation.

OFFENSE

JOE BUCK: When a hitter comes to bat against a pitcher he's never faced before, should he take a strike to see what the guy has or just swing at the first pitch he likes?

TONY LA RUSSA: This is a real problem we face all the time, especially with the way baseball has been going in the last few years. With as many young pitchers that are being introduced into the big leagues, you face this a lot. What we try to do is hedge it some. Besides the traditional scouting reports, we use as tape as much as possible of any performance the pitcher had done prior to pitching against your team. If your hitters have a look at a pitcher on tape, they'll get a feel for what his fastball does, what type of breaking balls he has, and what he used for another off-speed pitch. Now normally, when you go into the game, I think it's probably a good idea to take a look at what he throws. I think the qualification is: The game situation. For example, if you come up and there's nobody on base and you're trying to get things started, it's the perfect situation to just see a pitch or two from the guy so you know, and you can report back to your teammates. However, if you come up with the bases loaded, the most productive hitters are guys that are aggressive in game situations with men on base. So you may want to be ready to swing, even though you've never seen this pitcher before.

JOE BUCK: With a runner on second and nobody out, we hear about batters trying to hit to the right side to advance the runner to third. But what if the batter is a right-handed hitter and a dead pull hitter. Should he try to adjust or just swing away?

TONY LA RUSSA: This is a very good question and it's something you face, but hopefully not too much. You want to try to build on your complete hitters who can handle the bat depending on the situation. To have a hitter that is so pull conscious he can't hit the ball to the right side is a big negative as far as your offense goes. Somewhere during the course of the season, a very important run is going to be on second base with nobody out. If you can get him

OFFENSE

to third, your chance of scoring is about 74 percent. If you just let him swing away, it reduces your chance of a score. If you have a dead pull hitter and it's important to give up the out, you can bunt the guy, believe it or not. I don't care how big and strong the guy is and I don't care who he is, you can have him bunt the ball to the right side of the field and advance the runner. Many times that dead pull hitter is one of your power guys and you will let him swing away. You don't want him to sacrifice trying to hit for distance, so you don't take away his normal swing. What will commonly happen is that you may hit a long fly ball for an out but the runner will be able to tag and go. The other thing you look at is: Who is your runner is at second base? If it's a guy who is very quick, he can advance on almost anything. If it's a guy who is slow, you may want to give up the out and have the big pull hitter do something to the first base side.

JOE BUCK: What things can be done to try to help a player get out of a hitting slump?

TONY LA RUSSA: This is a great question, and it's something that you face every year with every hitter, except for the hitting machines. Everybody goes through a sluggish period or two or three, depending on how good a hitter you are, and you face that. I think the first thing you want to do is identify whether it started because of something mental or physical? What usually happens is, no matter where it started, it will become mental at some point. It's important to identify it. For example, if it's physical, the obvious physical issue is fatigue. There are times where a guy is played out, the bat is dragging, and to get the bat into the strike zone he'll start early, he'll start extending his swing, and he'll lose his quickness. All of those little adjustments will get him out of kilter. If it's physical or he's hurt, you want to do something to give him some time away. Maybe give him a break where he doesn't even take batting practice. Give him a couple days off. Usually though, work is the best way to get out of a slump, whether it's a hitting slump or a pitching slump. You may rest him a couple of days and then let him come out and take a lot of extra batting practice. You need to really simplify and work on some key fundamentals.

OFFENSE

JOE BUCK: Tony, what's the difference between the hit-and-run and the run-and-hit, and when would you use one or the other?

TONY LA RUSSA: The hit-and-run is technically when you send the runner and you instruct the hitter he must swing at the ball. The run-and-hit: The runner breaks from the bag and the hitter has the option of swinging if it's a good pitch to hit. However, if it's not a good pitch to hit, he can take it. When do you use one over the other? Obviously, the run-and-hit is used more with a good runner who has a likely chance to steal the base if there isn't a great pitch to throw on. What's a great pitch to throw on? A ball thrown down the middle is a great pitch to throw on. That's why you give the hitter the hit sign. If there is a fastball right down the middle, they've got a good chance to throw the runner out, so let him swing the bat. Maybe he gets a base hit or at least protects that runner. You use hit-and-run any time you want to be more aggressive than just bunting a guy over. You're trying to pick up at least one base. You think the one base can help you, and sometimes you'll strike gold, because the ball put in play will sneak through for a base hit, and you're looking at first and third. There are so many situations where you use that hit-and-run. I like to use hit-and-run instead of a bunt as often as I possibly can, because it's a more aggressive play than just giving up the out with the bunt.

JOE BUCK: Tony, is there a particular pitch count where it is best to put on a play such as the hit-and-run or a stolen base?

TONY LA RUSSA: I think generally, for a hit-and-run, most people will tell you it's when the hitter is ahead in the count. It's a little similar to the reasoning for a suicide squeeze. You feel it's more likely that the pitcher and catcher are thinking, "Throw a strike." A strike's thrown, the hitter puts the ball in play, and then you get the advance or maybe the ball gets through for a bigger inning. So with hit-and-run, very often you look for the count in your favor. Classics are 1-0, 2-1, 2-0. Now, the one thing you have to guard

OFFENSE

against is: If you've got an aggressive manager with some courage, and he knows that you're trying to hit-and-run, they will pitchout on you and defeat that inning with some courage and some judgment. So what you will see sometimes, to be unpredictable, is managers hit-and-run at unlikely counts like 0-1 or 1-1 just to keep the other side guessing and not just sitting on you. As far as the steal of a base, what you'd want to try to look for there is not so much the pitch as the type of break that he gets, with the unloading time of the pitcher. However, if you had to look for a pitch, any time you can think of a hard sinker or a breaking ball, that's usually the best pitch to try and run on.

JOE BUCK: Tony, when's your favorite count to try a hit-and-run?

TONY LA RUSSA: Why wouldn't you want to hit-and-run? The one thing that stops you is the other side knows you'll want to do it. You'll have these game situations where they read it just like you do. Is it a count they might pitchout? Where is it very difficult for them to pitchout? The best answer though is: When you think the ball will be thrown in the strike zone. What you want on a hit-and-run is for the ball to be thrown in the strike zone area where your hitter can put the ball in play, hopefully hard on the ground somewhere and find a hole. If you get that first and third, it can break open an inning. If you look at the different counts: 0-0 you never know where the pitch is coming; 1-0 probably has a better chance to be a strike. To me, the more the hitter sees the pitcher, the better read he gets on his release point and the type of stuff that he has. So if I had to pick one count, I would pick the 2-0 count, because by then he's already seen two pitches. At 2-0 they're almost always concentrating on throwing a strike. At 2-1 I don't think it's quite as good. However, 2-0 would be the count that I would pick. What you would also want to tell your hitter is: You're really in charge; don't just try to peck the ball somewhere. You want to take a nice forceful swing, hard on the ground.

OFFENSE

JOE BUCK: Tony, strikeouts don't advance runners, but they also don't result in double plays. How much does it really matter if a team strikes out a lot?

TONY LA RUSSA: I think it matters a lot. You have some great hitters who are very productive. I think in the end you look at the productivity of a hitter. One of the most famous examples is Reggie Jackson. He had big productive years and a lot of strikeouts. However, I think clearly that good hitting understands how devastating a strikeout can be. I think there are times with a runner on first — for example, it's a sinkerball pitcher and you're a slow runner, and I'm thinking, "Please don't hit it on the ground." I'd rather you strike out and have somebody else still swinging. However, almost every other time that you get into a situation, the strikeout does nothing to create positives for your offense. Nobody moves, and nobody can make an error on a ball that's not put into play. So almost always, it's very important to do something with two strikes that puts the ball in play. I think the strikeout happens when you are thinking, "I'm going to take three big swings at it." Number one, you very rarely hit the ball out when you're trying to take a big swing at it. Number two, big swings mean you come off the ball and your timing is affected.

JOE BUCK: Tony, hitters today are often given the hit sign on a 3-0 count. It used to be rare for even star players to swing on the count. Why the change in strategy?

TONY LA RUSSA: Here again I'm not sure how much the strategy has changed. I'll tell you what has really changed, and that's how many hitters are willing to hit 3-0. I do think, years ago, the book probably said that 3-0 was an automatic take, and there's been an evolution to where more and more good hitters are given the green light. I think just 15 or 20 years ago, a lot of the good hitters would love to see that 3-0 marshmallow right down the middle, and they'd really whack it. Here's the truth, in my opinion, about the hitters I've had in the last 20 years: More and more hitters do not like to hit 3-0. They just feel like they try to do too much. It bothers

OFFENSE

their thinking, their discipline, and their at bat. To me, what I try to do with the 3-0: First of all, you try to learn about your players, such as which guys are comfortable with it and which guys are not. Then, you try to use it as far as strategy. When does it produce something very special? Suppose you have the winning run at third base in a tie ball game in the bottom of the ninth inning, and the hitter goes 3-0. Why wouldn't you give him the 3-0 hit sign? The ball is there; he can just whack it and win the game right there.

JOE BUCK: **Tony, to you, what batting stance provides the best chance for success: an open stance, a closed stance or one that's squared up to the plate?**

TONY LA RUSSA: My answer would be: What happens after the stance? In other words .as the ball is thrown, as the pitch is made, what is your move toward the ball? That's why you see so many different varieties of stances from so many good hitters. The key is: As the ball is arriving at the plate, you get into a very good hitting position. Usually, that is where your front shoulder is tucked and going towards the pitcher and not away from him. If you put those things together, probably of the three stances, the one that's the most difficult to get into that good hitting position is the open stance, because you're open. You really have to get back closed to where you have a chance to attack the pitcher properly. The closed stance is one a lot of hitters have used and has the advantage where your shoulders are in there and driving, but it does have the possibility you're going to block yourself from really rotating and spinning and generating a lot of power. To me the best one is the square stance, but with that positive move to the pitcher, a lot like Mark McGwire's.

OFFENSE

JOE BUCK: Tony, during a game how often does a hitting coach talk to the starting players about particular things he sees from the opposing pitcher, and what about your bench players?

TONY LA RUSSA: That's a very interesting question, because this really changes from player to player, club to club, and hitting coach to hitting coach. In other words, there are a lot of different styles. Some hitting coaches do not like to talk much to their hitters during the game. Some hitters do not like to be talked to during the game. It really is something that you have to evaluate at the time. I think the healthiest situation is where you're carefully making comments. In other words, the hitting coach knows what the plan is going into the game. It could be the individual's plan. He knows the kind of approach he's going to take, what his mechanics are, and what he's going to be looking for from that pitcher. You have an idea what the pitcher is going to do against you. When you see something different — whether the hitter's different or the pitcher is different — then if you're carefully going to be able to talk to the guy and maybe give the hitter a certain pointer about his mechanics or about that pitcher, it's got to be healthy. The problem is that, if you overdo that, the hitter will start tuning you out, because you're talking too much. So it's really a work of art. Usually the less said the better, but a little bit is better than nothing.

JOE BUCK: Late in the game when a team needs a base runner, you constantly see hitters swinging at the first pitch. Little Leaguers are taught to take a strike in these situations, so why are big leaguers swinging away? And if the players won't do it, should a manager use a take sign to make sure?

TONY LA RUSSA: Absolutely. A manager can use a take sign anytime he thinks the game is not being played right. You will see cases, when you're behind in the game, where the hitter forgets about the team's need to produce base runners and to get a rally started so you can get back into this game. They just want to be selfish and generate their best shot at a base hit, so the first thing

OFFENSE

they see, they swing at. This is one of those areas where I think you have to be very careful when you talk about "the book." The book states: If you get behind, then take strike one. But, for example, if you face Dennis Eckersley and you've got three outs to tie him with one run down and you give him strike one, he's going to throw strike one in one of the first two pitches. That just means you've got two strikes left to save that at bat. I think what you really should do is watch very closely. If it's a pitcher who's struggling with his control, make him work. Make him throw a strike. If it's a guy who is going to throw strikes and is very dominating, you don't give up a strike because you only have a couple left to try and save it. Finally, where are you in the inning? If you are trying to get it started early, work the count to get it started. If you've got men on base, don't take a strike — do some damage.

JOE BUCK: Tony, with a good base runner on first and a good contact hitter at the plate, would you prefer to steal a base or attempt to hit-and-run?

TONY LA RUSSA: You would always prefer to steal a base because a hit-and-run, by definition, requires the hitter to swing. Suppose it's a pitch that's not in an area where he can hit it sharply, and he may just tap the ball someplace and he's an out. You pick up a base, but you've given up an out. The steal is always the better solution, because now he's in scoring position and this good contact hitter can hit that good contact somewhere, so a base hit might be a run. So why don't you always put the steal on? Because, and you can get Lou Brock to talk if you want, the running game is defended so much better than it used to be. I don't care who your base runner is — the guy could be the quickest or he may have 100 steals — but if this pitcher on the mound is unloading the ball quickly to the plate, if he's got a good, quick move to first base, or if he varies his times to the plate, then that stolen base is just not there. It's so easy to take a stolen base away nowadays that you're going to have to use a hit-and-run when they're defending the running game so much that your great base stealer just cannot run successfully. You have to get him moving only by putting him in play with a hit-and-run.

OFFENSE

JOE BUCK: Tony, explain the safety squeeze play and when you might use it.

TONY LA RUSSA: This is, I think, a very rare play and it can only be used, in my opinion, when your runner at third is one of those very good instinctive runners who has speed to match. A safety squeeze is when the hitter at the plate is showing the bunt, lays it down, and the runner at third reads the bunt off the bat to see if he can beat the ball to the plate. Usually, as the pitch is made, he breaks to the plate — not in a dash like a suicide squeeze, but he's breaking like he's taking a normal lead with a couple of hops and jumps towards the plate. If he sees the ball bunted slowly to first base, and the first baseman has not had a good break on it, then if he's quick enough and he's good enough to read it, he goes to the plate. It's very difficult for all of those things to come together. It's difficult for a runner to have that kind of instinct to make that kind of read. Usually it's not even worth practicing because it comes up so rarely. I think the safety squeeze is something you file away and you don't use very much.

JOE BUCK: Tony, we've heard on a previous show about the safety squeeze play. Explain the suicide squeeze and when you might use it.

TONY LA RUSSA: With the suicide squeeze, the elements are very straightforward, and it basically comes down to trying to predict when these things are all going to be there. The elements are: Runner at third and the hitter at the plate is not somebody you're confident can get the ball out of the infield with a base hit or a long enough fly ball to score the runner. You think about if we can bunt the ball successfully. Secondly, you have to anticipate whether the guy on the mound will throw the ball near the strike zone, so the ball can be laid down successfully. What are the things you look for? Look for when the count is such that the pitcher has to throw a strike. The one thing you're always fighting in this situation in the big leagues is that, if you run into a suicide squeeze situation with those elements where it's not a good hitter

OFFENSE

and the squeeze is possible, the other side knows it too. So they're looking very carefully, and they will be prone to either throw the ball out, throw the ball in, or maybe even pitchout. So a suicide squeeze is usually better early in the game, when it's not anticipated. Late in the game it's tougher, and you only use it if you think the hitter has no chance otherwise.

JOE BUCK: **Tony, say you have one of those true, good-field, no-hit kind of players. Are there ways to alter his approach to make him somewhat more effective at the plate?**

TONY LA RUSSA: Absolutely! And, first of all a good-field, no-hit guy can still help your team win, because defense is so important in winning baseball. Some of the things that you can do are: If you can get a guy to really stay inside the ball - you can forget pulling, because most of those good-field, no-hit guys don't have that extra little pop in their bat. Their line drives are kind of just a little looping liner. They don't have that little extra carry, and their ground balls don't have that little extra sting to get through. If you can have that guy stay inside the ball and use, for example a right-hand hitter, go from left-center to right field, you'll get some of those little flairs. You'll add some base hits to his game. Then you have to have him be very effective in all the little things that could make him help advance runners. For example, he should be an excellent bunter. You could really work on his base-hit bunting so he could bring the infielders in a little bit, and maybe slap something by. Then he has to be able to execute plays like the hit-and-run; he should never, ever swing and miss or hit a ball in the air if he's one of these types of hitters. You've got to execute that hit-and-run play. Last but not least, if he's not a very good hitter, what are pitchers going to do in a key situation? They're going to come right after you, so in an RBI situation, he would be very aggressive, take that fastball, and hit a little looping liner.

OFFENSE

JOE BUCK: **Tony, when a hitter squares around as if to bunt and then pulls back and tries to slap at the ball, they call it a slug bunt. Is that something you like to use a lot?**

TONY LA RUSSA: I think the only time with a player I like it is if you have a very fast runner who's also a very good bunter. Fernando Vina is a great bunter, so he really brings the infield in. You show a bunt, they start charging, and you can slap the ball. I would hesitate to think it would be a good play for a guy like Fernando Vina, because he's such a good hitter when he just stands there and takes a normal stroke. To me, it's a play that you would use with a guy who was not a really good hitter but has great speed. You're trying to maximize his speed, get the defense moving in, try to hit the ball side to side, and maybe get them a couple of extra hits. So that's a rare kind of player. What we do, and where you see it all the time in the National League, is with pitchers, because they are called upon to bunt in so many situations. An important part of defensive play in the National League is your bunt defenses. A lot of clubs defend the bunt so aggressively, and one way to neutralize that aggressive bunt defense, when the first and or the third baseman is crowding your pitcher, is to show a bunt and then have them bring it back and then go ahead and swing. If you do that a few times, you'll back that bunt defense enough to where, if you really wanted to bunt, you could come back and lay it successfully. So I like pitchers slug bunting.

BASE RUNNING

JOE BUCK: What is the third base coach thinking when he has a split second to decide whether to send a runner home on a ball hit to the outfield?

TONY LA RUSSA: If he has waited until the ball has been put in play to make that split second call, then he's very behind and will never really be a good third base coach. I think if you ask any third base coach, they are always anticipating. Very commonly, if you watch a third base coach, he's looking around, he's judging the depth of the outfielder, and he's reminding himself who can throw and who can't. During the course of the count, as the ball-strike count changes with the hitter, outfielders will change positions — some guy may shorten up; some guy may play more to pull or less to pull — so he is constantly watching that. He then evaluates the score, who the runner is, and how many outs. For example, if you're having a lot of trouble scoring and there's a runner at second. Even if he doesn't run very well, if you get a base hit with two outs, you almost always are going to send the runner because the chances of the next guy getting another base hit are probably not very good. What the third base coach is doing is trying to get his instincts and gut into the game. He's trying to figure all of these things so, when the ball is put into play, he'll recognize immediately if it's a ball at an outfielder and if it makes a lot of sense to try to gamble. How big of a gamble it is depends on the runner's speed and the outfielder's throwing arm.

JOE BUCK: Okay Tony La Russa, here's today's question. There's an old rule of thumb about base running that you should never make the first or third out at third base. What are your feelings on that rule and do you ever break it? Is there ever a situation where it makes sense to try it?

TONY LA RUSSA: I think the baseball book, the bible that has all these rules, you could really challenge several of them. But I think this is one rule that generally is very good and sound. As a general rule, you should teach your base runners: Don't make out one or out three at third base. Obviously, that means you have the runner

BASE RUNNING

stay at second if there are no outs, since you've got the makings of a good run-scoring inning. If you're at second base, you're already in scoring position. Are there times that you have an exceptional situation? Yes, I think so. I think if you're preaching to your club to be aggressive, aggressive, aggressive, and somebody pushes it one time, I don't think you want to exaggerate the rule and think it was wrong because you tried to run and it didn't work. Then your club would soon start to be conservative. Another good example of an exception to this rule is when I think trying to steal third base with two outs is a good play, assuming that it's a high percentage steal and most of the time you're going to make it. If you can get to third with two outs, there are a lot of ways to score, and there are several things the pitcher and catcher will not do to your hitter to prevent him getting a base hit. That's one case where you may risk making a third out at third base, and I think it's the exception.

JOE BUCK: Tell us more about why a runner should never make the first or third out at third base.

TONY LA RUSSA: Well, I heard it as recently as Opening Day. George Kissell was telling me in the dugout about a certain player he talked to regarding this rule and the reason why. It has been one of the things passed along in baseball since the turn of the century. I think that there is a lot of truth to it. The answer is: Because when you reach second base, you're in scoring position. Are you in as good a scoring position as you would be on third? The answer is no. If you could get to third with nobody out, that would be better. If you can get to third with two outs, as a matter of fact, you'd be better. I'm one of those guys that really believe that getting to third base with two outs is a good play. Sometimes we steal third with two outs even though the book and some people don't like that play. But the point is, if there's any risk in getting to third base with one or no outs, it's not worth the risk. If there's a chance that you might be thrown out, it's a bad play. If you're on second base with nobody out, there are ways to advance you to third and get you home. If you're on second, a base hit will usually score you. You

BASE RUNNING

don't have to rely on something else. I think that's one of those golden rules that really has a lot of truth to it, even a hundred years later.

JOE BUCK: Is it always good baseball to start a runner at first when the batter has a full count? When would you not start the runner?

TONY LA RUSSA: No, it's not always a good idea to send the runner. For example, if the runner at first is not your blazing speedster and the guy at the plate is a notorious strikeout guy. If the batter strikes out like he's been known to do, all you've created is a double play situation, because he will strike out, the catcher will throw to second and you're retired. What you want to do is try to figure out the probability that the ball is going to be put into play, especially if it's a ground ball. If you have a batter who handles the bat and puts the ball in play, you start the runner because you're going to pick up a base. If you've got a batter who swings and misses, you want to be more careful with that. If you have a player with good speed at first base, even if you have a swing-and-miss batter, start the runner. One special circumstance that you look at is first and third with nobody out, 3-2 count. Rarely is it a good idea to send the runner, because if he does strike out and you get a throw-through, you're going to have a double play with the guy left standing on third base. If you leave the runner on first there and the batter strikes out, you've got first and third, one out, and you still have an excellent chance to score.

JOE BUCK: Tony, a line drive into the gap bounces to the wall. How do the first and third base coaches help the hitter as he digs for a double or maybe a triple?

TONY LA RUSSA: Well, the first base coach can only tell the runner, "Don't give up on it, take your best shot, and make a good turn." The third base coach is really the traffic cop on this play. What you usually teach is: "Where is the ball hit?" If the ball is in

BASE RUNNING

front of the runner, especially if it's in left-center or on the left field line, it's really difficult for the player to watch the third base coach and watch the ball in the corner, so he must decide on his own. The third base coach can really help the runner if the ball is hit to right-center or especially in the right field corner. You don't want the runner looking back over his shoulder; that's just going to take away from his speed. We teach the runner to make a good turn and really run. If he can't pick up the ball, he looks to the third base coach, and the third base coach can help him. I think one of the most important things in this play is that when you leave the batter's box you have to be thinking, "I'm going to get two or three." You can't come out patting yourself on the back because you got a base hit and later on think, "Whoops, I can get an extra base," and then try to turn it on. You usually don't give up those extra steps and still get to the base safely.

JOE BUCK: Tony, with a runner on first base, there's a single to right. We often see the runner look over his shoulder out to right field as he rounds second. Since the play is not in front of him, shouldn't the runner pick up the third base coach instead? Is this a case of bad base running or has it become accepted practice in the big leagues?

TONY LA RUSSA: No, that's bad base running, and if you see that happen in any league, especially the major leagues, that's enough reason to really jump up, start booing, and criticize somebody, because that's just bad baseball. The way you're supposed to make that play is, as you're breaking from first base you want to build up a head of steam as quickly as you can. A very good base running strategy is to think two bases. If you hit the ball from the plate, you're trying to get to second base. That way you're really running hard and making a good turn. If you're on first, you're thinking third. If you're on second, you're thinking home. Being a runner on first base is hard, because if he has to look back over his shoulder, he's going to slow down. You're always taught that, as you get ready to make your turn, pick up your third base coach. He's the traffic cop. He gives you the "come on" or the hold. You're

BASE RUNNING

also told that, if the ball is in front of you, like if it's in center field or left field, then you don't look at the third base coach because you can make that call yourself. But, no question: ball in right field, just pick up the third base coach and keep running till he stops you.

JOE BUCK: Tony, do you believe in giving certain players a green light to steal?

TONY LA RUSSA: Absolutely. I think it's a very important part of the confidence that you try to show in a player. And if a player has good judgment on the bases, they know in the flow of the game when they're really feeling and reading a jump. Many times they can just tell by the pitcher's movements or even the way the catcher sets up. A lot of players like to run on breaking balls. If you try to control that from the bench, I think you miss a lot of tips. So the whole key really becomes, can you trust that player to run with a green light? One of the problems that has developed in modern baseball, since stats produce money, players try to produce a stolen base stat so they can go in there and say, "Hey, I want to make this much money because I had 25, 30, 40 steals." Well, they may have stolen 40 and gotten thrown out 30 times. What you really try to do is forget the money; try to see if the guy has good judgment. On our club, for example, a green light very often goes to Edgar Renteria who uses good judgment. Ray Lankford uses good judgment, and so does Jim Edmonds. Then what happens, whether they run or not, depends on how their legs feel.

JOE BUCK: So the bench doesn't always order a steal?

TONY LA RUSSA: I think the general rule is that you will have certain runners — on most clubs just a few — who have the green light when they get on base. That means that they use their own judgment to decide when they're going to run. And how you decide which of your runners get the green light? From experience. Does he have enough speed, but more does he have the savvy to read the situations when the stolen base is there and

BASE RUNNING

when they're taking it away. Even your best base runners, if the pitcher is really unloading quickly, will be thrown out. Sometimes, because of the game situation, it's foolish to try to push it. So it really comes down to: Does the runner have good judgment? On the Cardinals, a guy like Edgar Rentaria runs for a very high percentage. He has a green light a lot. I take the green light away when the game situation is such that I don't even want to risk it, because we're better off taking swings from the plate. For other players, you come in there and order it from the bench when you pick the pitch for them. If you don't trust their judgment or if you have a certain situation develop, the bench can order the stolen base for those runners.

JOE BUCK: **How to you determine which players to give a green light, and are there instances where you revoke this green light privilege in certain game situations?**

TONY LA RUSSA: The answer fans probably expect would be that the green light is given to players with speed, but I think that is only one factor. The most important reason you give a green light to any player is judgment. By that I mean you can have a guy who does not run well, and you can give him a green light every time he gets on base all year long. That's because he will know those few times that it's all in place for him to steal a base — for example, when the pitcher has forgotten about him, he's slow to the plate, or he's letting you get a great jump. Vice versa, you can have a player with terrific speed who has terrible judgment — running against pitchers who are unloading the ball very quickly or telegraphing his lead to where the other side sees it and pitches out with regularity. To me, you want to read the game situation and you want to read your personnel. There are certain times when it would be crazy to try to push a steal because you just don't have that out potential to give up. But mostly, what you want to do is see whether your runner has good judgment. The idea is to run for a high percentage of success, not build a big stolen base total and be caught stealing many times.

BASE RUNNING

JOE BUCK: Tony, in general what is the best pitch count to try to steal a base?

TONY LA RUSSA: Good question. Here are some of the factors that I think would come into the answer: "When do you think the pitcher would be the most distracted from concentrating on the hitter? When do you think the other side is not paying as much attention to him? What types of pitches does he have?" More than anything else, everybody times the pitch release to the point of arriving at the plate. What pitches take the longest to get there? Now if you put all that together, I think if I had to pick one count, I would pick the 1-2 count, because that's probably the situation where the pitcher's thinking that he's got the hitter at a disadvantage and he's going to try and wipe him out. With the 0-2 count, a lot of times you waste that pitch with a fast ball. A 1-2 pitch very often is a breaking ball. If you can run on a curve ball or split finger, you've got a much better chance to steal because you're adding a couple tenths of a second to your running time toward second base. The other thing that you look for: If the pitcher has a dynamite sinker, the sinker is very tough for the catcher to catch and bring all the way up to the throwing position.

JOE BUCK: Tony, sometimes it seems obvious to everyone in the ballpark when a base runner's going to steal, and sometimes he does. Why can't the pitchers and catchers get a guy in that situation?

TONY LA RUSSA: Good question, and if you absolutely knew, then one way to defend is with a pitchout. That's why you see pitchouts in certain situations. But if you really watch the base runner that everybody knows is going to run, he doesn't run every time you think he's going to run. They mix up their counts, so the pitchout is not the most efficient way to stop that base runner. The most efficient way is for the pitcher to vary his time to the plate. In other words, when the pitcher delivers he should not always have the same set routine so the runner can anticipate and get a better

BASE RUNNING

jump. Secondly, the time taken from unloading the pitch to the catcher receiving it can be so quick that the catcher has a chance to throw him out. What you will see too often is they do not defend the running game with the pitcher. He has a set routine that's easy to read or his time to the plate is so slow that no matter how much the catcher tries to get rid of it quickly and makes a perfect throw, the runner's going to be safe. I think the best answer when you know he's going: Pitchout. But since you don't always know he's going, it's even better to have your pitcher ready to defend the running game with a quick time to the plate and varying his times.

JOE BUCK: **Tony, if you've decided to have your runner at third base steal home, what did you see from the other team that led you to that decision?**

TONY LA RUSSA: What's not in this question is whether it is the straight steal by the runner at third or is it the back end of the double steal? I'm going to explain the double steal here in a minute, because that's the one you see more frequently. It's very rare nowadays that you see the straight steal with the runner at third base. The only way you would see that straight steal is if the pitcher is in his windup and his delivery is so slow — and you're timing it — that the runner can take a break and score before he gets the ball to the plate. Most pitchers defeat that very easily by going into the stretch. What you do see, though, is the steal at home at the back end of the double steal. You send the runner at first and you hope that the catcher's throwing the ball through. The runner at first stops as the catcher unloads the ball to second base. The runner at third breaks for home, and he beats the relay from the second baseman or the shortstop. You do that when you think you know for sure that the ball is going through. Maybe you look for an infielder who doesn't have the strongest arm on a relay back to the plate so you can beat the exchange and be safe. I think that's what you look for.

BASE RUNNING

JOE BUCK: Would you tend to attempt a double steal late in a game or early?

TONY LA RUSSA: There are two types of double steals. You're talking about first and second where you steal second and third, or you're talking about first and third where the runner at first leads off, the runner at third tries to steal home, then the guy at first gets into second base as the throw comes home. Normally, you only try a double steal when the defense gives it to you. For example, with the first and second situation, that could be anytime in the game if the infielders are backing off. If the pitcher on the mound is forgetting about the base runners — we call it one-looking or two-looking — every time he looks back there, he looks with one look and then throws the ball to the plate. As soon as he looks away from you, you can start running. If his time to the plate is not quick, you can get those bases. So I think the answer for first and second is: When it's there for you. The double steal, where you're talking about stealing home, that's a tougher breed of cat because there are times where you know the other side is worried about that runner on third coming home. They're just not going to give up that steal of home, so you're not going to consider it because they're going to defend it with either a fake or the crash play or something like that. So the double steal of home usually works better early in the game.

JOE BUCK: What sort of situation would be ideal to try a double steal?

TONY LA RUSSA: Well, there are two types of double steals, right? There's first and second where you're stealing second and third, and there's first and third where you're trying to steal second and home. Just take the first one, when you're trying to steal second and third. Obviously, if you're at first and second and you can get second and third, it's always worth it to try because a base hit is two runs instead of one. So the things you look for are: Do you have enough speed both places, and is the defense allowing you the bases? In other words, if they're really crowding your

BASE RUNNING

runner at second, or even first, where they could throw behind the lead runner, then you don't want to risk it because you've already got a runner in scoring position. The first and third double steal is one that's a gamble, and you look for certain keys. Do you think that they're going to throw the ball through? And if you think the ball's going to be thrown through to second base, the classic double steal is the runner on first breaks, he draws the throw, he stops, the runner on third breaks for home as the throw's being made to second base. What you try to do in a game is try to anticipate whether you think the ball's going through or they've got one of the fake defenses.

JOE BUCK: Tony what's a delayed steal and when do you use it?

TONY LA RUSSA: If you're a second baseman or shortstop with the coverage responsibility of second base, out of the corner of your eye you're watching the runner take his lead. If he breaks as the pitcher makes his first move, you know it's a straight steal or a hit-and-run, and you start moving in the direction of second base. But if you see a runner just take his first hop or two like a normal lead, then your attention is diverted to the plate. You're not aware the runner is still going unless you look back again like you were taught to pick up the runner after his first hop — some people teach two hops, we teach one and a go — then you see him running, and you still get to the bag and you'll be there in time, if the catcher has not fallen asleep. Why would you use it? You'll see the middle infielder, or whoever has the coverage responsibility, drop his head when the pitch is thrown. In other words, he's not making that second check of the runner to see if he's still going. The middle infielders may be so far off the bag — they may be covering a hole at short and the other hole at second — that you can visualize the cover guy taking the throw on the run. Last but not least, the best time to use it is when you have a runner who doesn't have steal speed, so they'll relax a little bit defensively, and he'll take that delay and catch them napping. A delayed steal is useful in that situation.

DEFENSE

JOE BUCK: What positions would you be willing to play someone regularly who is good with a glove but not much of a hitter, and on the other hand, are there positions where you would sacrifice defense to get more offense?

TONY LA RUSSA: The classic book on baseball is right on time here. The middle of the diamond is very key defensively. You will win more games by stopping the other club first than you will by having to outscore them day after day. The catcher, the second baseman, the shortstop and the center fielder are all guys with big defensive responsibilities, and it's very important that you be solid at those positions. If you had to choose the offensive versus the defensive guy, I think you would choose defense at those spots. There are a few other points, though. You want to be defensive at all positions where you can. The ball will go to third and first, left and right. Another little take-off on that, which I was taught from veteran managers, is: If you have a game where you know it's going to be tough to score and you think your pitcher is going to give up some runs, then defense is not the first priority. Maybe you may have an offensive player that you might play at short or second or catcher or center. What you want to do is start that guy and try to get the jump in the game. Try to take the lead and come back in the second half of the game with your strongest defense.

JOE BUCK: Okay Tony La Russa, here's today's question. A center fielder's main job is to cover ground and take charge. What's the main difference then between playing left field and playing right field?

TONY LA RUSSA: I think in left and right, first of all, as opposed to center, these are guys that you look to for different type of offense and more offense. I think the important differences are the strength of the throwing arm. You know that in right field you have a lot of tough throws. You have that very important throw from right to third base to prevent the runner from going from first to third. You also have a chance to throw guys out at the plate. In left field, your throws are shorter to third, especially to that base, so

DEFENSE

you'll very often have the stronger throwing arm in right field, and not so strong in left. However, if you had the perfect situation, you would try to put a left-handed thrower playing right field and a right-handed thrower playing left field. When they move towards the line, they can easily make that pivot and throw and don't have to throw across their body. If you want to isolate one answer, the difference between left and right should be the strength of the throwing arm.

JOE BUCK: Okay Tony La Russa, here's today's question. How do you decide when to use late-inning replacements that strengthen your defense but may weaken your offense?

TONY LA RUSSA: I think the key is whether you have the lead or not, and one of the beauties of being ahead in the game is that, if you can stop the other club, you're the winner. You don't have to do anything else. So I think defensive replacements are something you only consider when you're ahead. The other thing I think is worth mentioning is: It's probably the toughest job in baseball to be a defensive replacement. People talk about pinch-hitting being so tough. and it is, it's a real difficult, demanding, specific-type job. But then you talk about an infielder who's supposed to go in and play third base or second or whatever. If you're a defensive guy and that's your contribution to the club, the pressure on you is to go in there late, and if you make any kind of miscue, it's going to really affect your team's chance to win. I think that's the toughest job in baseball. So you try to have a good defensive club and a good offensive club so you don't get into that hassle. Any time that you have to make defensive changes, you're really running the risk of the other club coming up and tying the game. The big threat you might face is if you have a big left fielder that you took out for defense. When his turn to bat comes up in the extra innings, he's not in the game anymore, and that's a real difficult situation for a ball club. Try to avoid it.

DEFENSE

JOE BUCK: **Okay Tony La Russa, here's today's question. To you, which is more important in an outfielder's throwing arm: accuracy or strength?**

TONY LA RUSSA: By far, the answer is accuracy. In fact, you can go back over the recent history, center field for example, and look at clubs that played in the post season with a center fielder that did not really have a strong throwing arm. But if you have the ability to get to the ball quickly and unload it and get it into the glove of a cutoff man, a coach will stop a runner. If you have this real strong arm and you're constantly missing the cutoff man or you're throwing the ball erratically, usually that means a couple of extra bases for the offense. The guy that you're trying to throw out makes the base that he's going to, and the other guy that got the base hit takes an extra base. So what you really try to emphasize with your outfielders is get the ball to the cutoff man. Accuracy is much more important than strength.

JOE BUCK: **Okay Tony La Russa, here's today's question. It is often said that a catcher "calls a good game." What exactly does that mean?**

TONY LA RUSSA: I think that's one of the least credited jobs after a win. Many times you look who got the big hits or if the pitcher had pitched well, but we always try to make it a point to give the catcher credit. Calling a good game is a combination of understanding what hitters you're trying to get out, what their strengths are and then taking the pitcher that's pitching that inning, whether it's the starter or reliever, and pitting that guy's strengths against the hitter's weakness. You've got to remember what you did early in the game, because you may have to set up a hitter for something later in the game. Suppose you had been getting him out with fastballs inside in the first couple of times at bat, but the third or fourth time he may look in. A good catcher will then recognize this and pitch him away, then change the pattern later in the game. The other part of calling a good game is checking your pitcher's frame of mind, because you'll see a pitcher

DEFENSE

start to get excited, or you'll see him start to get agitated or distracted because things aren't going well. That's why a trip to the mound by the catcher can be so important. So if you see a well-pitched game, it's a combination of the catcher putting the right numbers down as far as calling pitches and also tracking the pitcher's frame of mind.

JOE BUCK: **Okay Tony La Russa, here's today's question. Why do baseball people stress the importance of being strong up the middle?**

TONY LA RUSSA: You look at any good baseball team, in fact almost any good athletic competition, and the number one priority is stopping your opponent first, and then you get to the offensive part of the game. In baseball, if you're going to stop the other club, it begins with the pitcher, the catcher, your second baseman, shortstop, and your center fielder. If you look at the percentage of balls that are put into play, they're going somewhere from left center to right center — from short to second. That's where most of the balls get hit and will have most of the plays. Your pitcher's obviously throwing the ball so he's involved in every play that you start. So the old truism about sacrificing some offense to get quality defense at positions up the middle is a good way to build a ball club. There is one better way, and that is to have a truly well-rounded player, such as a guy who plays up the middle who is good defensively and contributes offensively too. Then you've got something special, like a Barry Larkin or Craig Biggio, and you know what Ozzie's been throughout his career. He's hit high into the .200's and .270's - .280's — not just great defense. That's really what you look for. But if you had to make a choice, I'd take defense over offense up the middle.

DEFENSE

JOE BUCK: What are the different skills you look for in a shortstop and a second baseman? Why is it that some players can play both positions and others can't?

TONY LA RUSSA: I think there really is one major difference and that's the strength of the throwing arm. Other than that, a good shortstop and second baseman share skills. You should have the ability to make the routine play, which means you have nice soft hands and you get yourself in good fielding position. You should have at least average range; anything above average just means you increase the number of balls you get to. Looking at what Ozzie did for us for many years, that's way above average range. But you can win if you make the routine play all the time. So I think the strength of the throwing arm is the difference. The shortstop is required to go deep in the hole. It's a very difficult throw to make, and it requires a strong arm. The second baseman can get away with flipping the ball to first base. You really only see his arm called upon when you have the double play, and that is where a strong arm really pays off. But you can be quick with your release and make that up. So I think the strength in the arm is the big difference.

JOE BUCK: Tony, other than experience playing together, what makes a good double play combination?

TONY LA RUSSA: Experience playing together is an important thing to start with. Playing together is very important, because everybody has their own style. The most important keys are the types of feed. What you really teach to the infielder that's receiving the ball is it's much more important for you to give the pivot man something that he can handle and get rid of effectively than it is to try to really speed up and make a poor feed. The good double play combinations are guys that really catch the ball cleanly and show the ball to their pivot partner. In other words, some players hide the ball and the guy who's making the pivot doesn't get a real good read on it, so he isn't in a good position to use the footwork, to make the throw and avoid the runner. A good double play

DEFENSE

combination is two guys who understand that. when catching the ball, it's necessary to get rid of it quickly, but much more important, show the ball to your pivot partner and give him a good throw. Let the guy who is making the pivot have something to work with, because he's got the big responsibility — making a good throw and avoiding the runner.

JOE BUCK: Okay Tony La Russa, here's today's question. How do a good shortstop and a good second baseman complement one another? Can you talk about the relationship between the two middle infielders?

TONY LA RUSSA: I think the most obvious time they interact is when they make double plays. When you think about a double play, most often the first basic is that the player who receives a ground ball makes a good throw, because the player who's making the pivot is the one that has to make the toughest part of the play. He's got a runner that's sliding into him, plus he has to catch the ball and throw it. When you see a good double play combination, the second baseman and shortstop really get to know each other and they'll read different ground balls. When the ground ball is taking the receiver towards the bag, then the player who's going to make the pivot knows that he's likely to lead him or go the other way. If the player is going to catch a ground ball away from the bag and have to plant himself and throw, then he's likely to throw the ball where it protects the pivot man from the runner who's coming in. So I think the double play is one place that you really see that interaction. Another one is when they have to cover the base on a potential hit-and-run or a steal, and they always communicate who's got the coverage. Relays and cutoffs — one guy goes out as the relay, the other guy's a trailer. They help each other onto third with the ball and then home with the ball. So it really is one of the places where there is a lot of teamwork.

DEFENSE

JOE BUCK: Okay Tony, here is today's question. In a tight late-inning ball game, what is the biggest factor in determining whether to hold a runner at first base?

TONY LA RUSSA: I think the question answers itself. If you have a tight game, you always have to hold that runner on. In fact, that is why, when there is a legitimate stolen base threat, you pay so much attention to throwing over and stepping off and maybe even pitching out, because that is like giving the hitter a double. Say he singles, you let him steal second, and that "double" and another base hit will beat you. I think it really comes down to: How important is that run? Who is the runner? Can he legitimately steal the base? Then the next factor is: When the count gets very deep, such as the classic 3 and 2, do you hold the runner on or do you play behind them? Most times, if it is a right-handed hitter, I think you hold them on because the ball is not likely to go to that hole. You are just giving the runner an extra two or three steps that he might be able to score on a gapper. If it is left-handed hitter, you probably want to play behind or take the hole away.

JOE BUCK: In a sacrifice bunt situation, every infielder is on the move with the pitch. How does the defense decide who's covering each base?

TONY LA RUSSA: The easy one is the runner on first base. For that one, the shortstop is going to cover second, the second baseman will come over to cover first, and you want your first and third basemen and pitcher converging on the bunt. The catcher is going to come out from his position. Where you really have some choices is the runner on first and second bunt situation. That's one where you have both sides of it. On one side, it's very difficult to bunt with the force play at third base. You can really pinch the hitter/bunter where it's not an easy bunt to execute. By the same token, if you're pinching, you really have some big areas of exposure. And if for some reason the hitter is swinging away or if you do something more aggressive, even like a hit-and-run, the ball could sneak through and you can really turn that into a big

DEFENSE

inning. So, first and second, nobody out, most clubs have at least three or four variations on which infielders are coming in what areas and who is covering what bags. The Cardinals have four different defenses that we will typically use with a runner at first and second with nobody out.

JOE BUCK: **With a lead late in the game, do you prefer to have your first and third basemen guard the lines or play more straight away?**

TONY LA RUSSA: Here's another one of those second-guess delights. I think that classic baseball book rules state that, late in the game, you are supposed to protect the lines. I think the way that I was taught, and it seems to make sense, is that you want to play the situation. You want to play the type of pitcher and type of hitter. For example, if you've got somebody whose really throwing the ball hard and you've got a hitter with a slow bat, why would you want to play the third baseman down the third base line? You're just opening up a hole for a lot of base hits. We try to look at where the ball is most likely to be hit. You try to learn, depending on your pitcher, where the ground balls are hit. For example, a left-hand slider is often enough hit by a right-hand hitter down the third base line. So what you should do is play the shortstop to pull in the hole and the third baseman has got to play the line. Now, with a Dennis Eckersley, who threw hrowing a fastball and slider away from a right-hander, he doesn't get pulled down the line very much, so you may protect the hole a little bit. So it really depends on the type of hitter and the type of pitcher. If you have a dead pull hitter, play the line. If you've got a guy who hits in the opposite field, don't play that line.

DEFENSE

JOE BUCK: *The score is tied in the seventh inning or later. There's a runner on third with less than two out. How do you decide whether to play the infield in or leave it back at regular depth?*

TONY LA RUSSA: You're going to be tempted to play the infield in. If you are deep in the game, that run has a very good chance of beating you, especially if you look at modern day baseball. Most clubs are set up with really good bullpens. You let them get the lead against you and you may have the best pitcher on that staff trying to get the last three or four outs against you. Normally, the infield would be in. I think an important point to make about this part of the baseball game is: What does infield "in" mean? How is that defined? One of the keys that you look for here is: Who is the runner at third base? For example, Tom Pagnozzi does a lot of great things, but he's not a great runner. If he's at third base versus Royce Clayton, your infield "in" is not the same for both players. So you can play your infield "in" for a guy like Tom and the shortstop may be halfway between the back infield grass and the front infield grass. I think you want to adjust depending on the speed of the runner, but your thought at the seventh inning or later is, if that run will beat you, you're going to stop that run at the plate. You have to adjust the depth.

JOE BUCK: *Tony, who sets the defense, you or one of your coaches?*

TONY LA RUSSA: I think the answer to that is: Anything that comes down to a final responsibility, the manager has to assume it. For example, if we get beat in the game and everybody agrees that the outfielder was out of position, you're not going to be able to say, "Well, look man, I told one of my coaches to take care of it." Or, "I really told the middle infielder to look over his shoulder to be sure the center fielder was in place." It's the manager's responsibility, but it's a process that we all get involved with. Setting the defense is a particular pet of Dave Duncan. He does a lot of manual work, not computer work, to see where the ball goes

DEFENSE

against our pitchers; each particular pitcher from each particular hitter. Rene Lachemann also keeps charts that we can double check. We can look at our advance stuff, and then we will talk. On our ball club last year, Dave McKay tracks the outfield positioning; Carney Lansford tracks the infield positioning. And as the manager, I'm aware of Dave and what he's talking about. I watch the game, watch our pitcher and their hitter, and I've got nothing else to do, so I just kind of watch them. You'll see me shift guys here and there. So we're all involved with it, but the final call has to be the manager's.

JOE BUCK: Tony, can you defend against a player who's good at stealing bases?

TONY LA RUSSA: Yes, I think you can definitely defend against a player who's good at stealing bases. You may not be able to defend a player who's great at it. For example, there are some guys who have such explosive speed and so much judgment, there's almost nothing you can do to stop them. However, if you just look at all the people who are involved in defending that play, the pitcher is the first key. If he will have a quick delivery to the plate, where he doesn't take a lot of time unloading, that's good defense against a stolen base. If he has a good pick-off move, a nice quick snap throw, that will shorten the runner's lead by a step or two. The other factor that's very important is to vary his times to the plate as far as unloading. You will see some pitchers get into a routine. They come set, and you can almost count, "One, two, throw." A runner does that; he counts, "One, two," and starts running. You'll see that stolen base some times, where the runner is halfway to second because he just guessed the pitcher's timing. So pitchers need to vary their timing. The other area you work with is your catcher, by making sure he has a quick release and an accurate throwing arm. You can also defend with a lot of pitchouts. That's something that some runners get very leery about. They get very embarrassed by being thrown out with a pitchout, and you can take away a couple pitches from them.

DEFENSE

JOE BUCK: Tony, predominantly, would a runner steal the base off the pitcher or off the catcher?

TONY LA RUSSA: Most of the time in the big leagues, I think the answer is the pitcher. Most clubs cannot afford to have a catcher who does not throw well. If you literally are stealing bases off the catcher, he better have some kind of offense going for him. Almost always, the stolen bases come because the pitcher doesn't do the keys. He's very slow to the plate. He's very routine in his counts as far as delivering the ball to the plate. He doesn't vary his timing. The other thing you see that's a real crime is that his pick-off move takes so long to get the ball to first base. He's very slow with his feet. He has this very long arc in his throw to first base, so you can get off ten to twelve feet and still get to first base easily. However, once in a while, the catcher is not strong-armed or is not accurate. Or you will hear the catcher's really having problems throwing, and you'll run on the catcher. But usually, the pitcher is the one who's got the first opportunity to defend the stolen base. If you see a lot of stolen bases and you hear somebody saying, "They really run on this catcher", check the pitcher out because it's almost always his fault and his responsibility to do something about it.

JOE BUCK: Tony, in an all-or-nothing situation, in a tie game, last inning, nobody out and bases loaded, you bring the outfielders in. What advantage does that give you and how far in do you bring the outfielders?

TONY LA RUSSA: The consideration there is: The runner at third beats you if he scores, so you want to look at his speed. You want to look at the strength of the outfielder's throwing arm. And the whole point is that, if you catch the ball, you have to be sure that you can throw the runner out at the plate. If you take two steps past that point, and the guy scores, you're too deep. So you'll see a guy with a strong arm much deeper than a guy who doesn't have a good arm. But the whole idea is that, if you catch the ball safely, you've got to be able to throw this runner out. If a guy doesn't run well, you play deeper. If he's faster, you play closer. The other

DEFENSE

consideration, though, is that most line drives you can get to in a hurry, and sometimes the runner will break and maybe not get a great jump. More than anything else, it's where you have to be to catch it and throw the runner out — your arm, his speed. The other thing you can do sometimes, and it doesn't happen very much at all anymore, is to bring in the fifth infielder and go with two outfielders. However, the whole point is, if it's a deep enough fly ball, you lose anyway.

JOE BUCK: **Tony, little league shortstops and second basemen like to hold the runner on second base while the pitcher comes set in the stretch position. Some coaches insist that pitchers never deliver a pitch until the infielders get back into position. But major league pitchers often pitch with the middle infielders just a few strides from second base. Is that a good strategy or do more hits result because the infielders are out of position?**

TONY LA RUSSA: One of the situations you face in a lot in Major League Baseball is you can't have everything. You have to take your choice of which is your best chance to win. I'll give you a classic situation that this question illustrates, which is when you have a runner on second base. For example, there's one out, and if he gets to third via a stolen base, his chances to score are greatly improved. If he is a very good base runner who could steal that base easily, you have to do a lot of things to defend that stolen base. By moving your second baseman or shortstop close to the runner, this keeps him close to the bag and prevents his stealing a base. What that does is open up the second or shortstop area and you might have a hit slip through there. If you want to protect against the hit and you move the player off, then the runner steals third, and any kind of fly ball or little ground ball might score him. I think what you have to do is figure whether the runner can steal third. If he's going to steal third, how much would it hurt you?

DEFENSE

JOE BUCK: Tony, outfielders sometimes run into each other while calling for the same ball. Aren't there priorities in the outfield if the ball is hit between two players?

TONY LA RUSSA: Absolutely. The priority belongs to the center fielder, who is the quarterback. He's the guy that takes charge of the balls. The only people that run into each other are the center fielder and the left fielder, or the center fielder and the right fielder. This usually happens when communication gets disrupted in some of these Major League parks. With all the noise as you're chasing the ball, or sometimes given the condition of the lights, whether it's a day game or night game, the ball is not that easy to track. As you're focusing on that ball, you only have this sense of the side fielder coming at you and a potential for collision. Now, one player is calling it or they're both communicating with each other. However, both players may not hear a thing, so most of the collisions happen because they can't tell who's calling the ball. You're talking about the real in-between situation where they're both about to get to it. That's the one that creates the biggest problem. You almost can't avoid it. Normally, we do drills where the center fielder goes in front and the side fielder goes behind. That way you try to avoid the collisions. However, the biggest problem sometimes is having these players hear each other in a ballpark with a lot of noise.

JOE BUCK: Tony, could teams try to intimidate low average hitters and hitters who consistently hit to one part of the field by playing dramatic defensive shifts?

TONY LA RUSSA: Absolutely. Look at how teams are defending Mark McGwire in the infield for example. Almost everybody now is playing their second baseman up the middle or even on the shortstop side, and the shortstop is way in the hole. So if there's a dramatic potential or a tendency to hit the ball in one area, you're obviously going to group your defense there. There are some hitters that just fan the ball to the opposite field with not much power. In those situations, the right fielder will play over toward the

DEFENSE

line in shallow, and the center fielder will play over in right center. However, if you're talking about exaggerating, you don't take the left fielder and put him in a roving position between the center fielder and the right fielder. This is because there isn't anybody who survives in the big leagues that has that kind of exaggeration — where almost every ball he puts in play is going to go to one small area. I think the answer is that, if you had somebody that was really exaggerated and placing the ball in a certain area, that's why you do the charts and you definitely try to align your defense that way. Not many hitters survive in the big leagues with that type of approach, and therefore you don't have that come up very often.

JOE BUCK: **Tony, with a man on first and a left-handed hitter at the plate, do you have the shortstop or the second baseman cover the possible stolen base attempt or does it depend on how you're trying to pitch to the hitter?**

TONY LA RUSSA: It definitely depends on how you are trying to pitch to the hitter and the type of situation that you're in. A lot of left-handed hitters will see the first baseman holding the runner and they'll have that big hole, so they'll try to roll that ball over in the hole. If you think he's trying to pull the ball, your shortstop will cover. If you've got somebody that's definitely pitching away and has good command and you can see that the hitter is just trying to play the ball to the middle, then you might want your second baseman to cover. It really depends on the situation. Most of the time, with a left-handed hitter, you have to protect the right side with your second baseman, and the shortstop will cover. The only thing that would make a difference there is if you play the situation. You will get into some counts and game situations — score and what not — where the hit-and-run is a factor or the stolen base is a factor. If you really believe the ball is being thrown away to the left-handed hitter and the runner takes off, the ball will be put into play to the left side. So I think the answer is to play the situation, change it occasionally, but most of the time, the shortstop is going to cover.

DEFENSE

JOE BUCK: Tony, there's a runner on first and a ball is hit back to the pitcher. How does he decide whether to throw to first or second, and what if there's a runner on third?

TONY LA RUSSA: If the runner's on first and you get a ball back to you, a lot of it just depends on how comfortable you feel when the ball's in your glove. In other words, sometimes as a pitcher, you're very close to that hitter. A lot of these guys are off balance when they catch the ball in their glove. They're not in great position to make a more difficult throw to second base. So a lot of times you will see a pitcher who fields a ball back to the mound elect to throw the ball to first, and it has everything to do with how he caught the ball and how he had to regroup to make a throw. If you catch the ball well and you've got yourself under control, the throw to second base obviously keeps the runner out of scoring position. If you have a runner on first and third, it all depends on the game situation. The only way to answer that is to talk about the game situation. If the runner at third is the one that's going to tie or beat you or is very important, you throw the ball to the plate: you get him out rather than try for the double play. Is the guy who hit the ball a real double play threat? If he's a slow runner, you throw to second base and you're out of the inning. So it all depends on what the game shows you.

JOE BUCK: Tony, what factors do you consider when deciding whether to bring the entire infield in or just the first and third baseman?

TONY LA RUSSA: It all depends on how much that run at third hurts you. You have to weigh that against the possibility of opening up a big inning. In other words, if you bring in the entire infield and the guy at the plate gets one through there, a little pop up over the infield or a ground ball that sneaks through, now you've got the run scored and you've got an extra base runner. So normally what you're looking at is: How bad that run at third hurts you. If it's a real tough run, you bring the infield in. The other thing to talk about here is the infield depth, because if you don't have a very good

DEFENSE

runner at third, you can really have some fun by bringing your entire infield in some, but not all the way. Often, that will spook the other side, because they know he doesn't run well and they won't send him. Normally, what you want to do is play the off side in. So, if you have a right-handed hitter, you might as well play the first baseman in. Every once in a while, in a tough situation, you'll have a ball hit kind of off the end of the bat where if you had played them back, the run would have scored. If you play them in, he can stop that run from scoring. You almost never have a ball hit past the off side corner guy because he was playing in.

JOE BUCK: Tony, you're winning late in a one-run game. There's a fast runner on first and a light-hitting batter at the plate. Are you more inclined to play your outfielders deeper, making sure an extra base hit doesn't score the run or do you play them closer and try to take away the hit?

TONY LA RUSSA: Now this is a great question because I think it gives you a chance to think about what is your best chance to win. I think that all the manager is trying to do for the club is put them in the best position to win. So you're trying to evaluate that all the time, but you also understand there are no guarantees. That's why I see more managers trying to protect themselves, cover their butt, end up costing themselves a good chance to win, and sooner or later they lose their job. For example, if you have, as this question says, a light-hitting infielder or a light-hitting player at the plate, you have to play your outfield a little shallower. However, if he happens to catch one of his rare line drives that's hit between the fielders and carries all the way to the wall, the guy at first scores and somebody says, "Well the book says that you play the outfield back on a no double situation." Then you're going to get criticized for it. But I tell you what, you will lose a hell of a lot more games by playing the outfield back when you have a guy just popping a ball a little over the infield than if you played them according to how he's supposed to hit the ball.

DEFENSE

JOE BUCK: Tony, we've talked a little bit about it, at least during spring training earlier in the year, that you may be having the second baseman charging this year in bunt situations. What benefits does this give your defense and where did you get this idea?

TONY LA RUSSA: There's a couple of clubs that use it. It's not a frequent play, but it's not so unusual it's never been used. The reason we would do it, in a situation where you're really sure that the hitter is bunting, is almost always because of the pitcher. It's a pitcher who does not handle the bat well. The other side really doesn't want to let this guy swing when you're aggressively defending the bunt, because he might just tap something right at a player for a double play. So in that bunt defense, one of the options is to have your first baseman be very aggressive. If you think about Mark and the problems that he has with his back and everything, it makes it very tough and risky for the St. Louis Cardinals to try to aggressively defend the bunt with our first baseman. That's asking Mark to do something that he shouldn't do, can't do, so we're going to use the second baseman at times with a Vina to take that same bunt defense.

JOE BUCK: Tony, there are obviously several ways to defend against a bunt, so how do you as a manager decide which to use at some given point during a game?

TONY LA RUSSA: Just as there are several ways to defend the bunt, there are several ways offensively to defeat the bunt defense. What you try to do is think along with what's your best strategy in that situation. By that I mean, I was raised — some managers believe this, but maybe others do not — that on offense, I believe in being very aggressive, taking some chances and taking some risks. I think aggressiveness on offense produces extra runs. However, on defense, I think it makes more sense to be very fundamental, very basic, take the outs that they try to give you. What you need to do to decide on bunt defenses is to realize the situation. For example, the classic one is first and second, nobody

DEFENSE

out: Do you try the wheel play or the crash play where the first, third and pitcher are charging right towards the hitter? That can be very effective if he's bunting, but if they switch, and most teams teach the pitcher not to bunt into that crash but to slug bunt where you drill a ball by a charging infielder or a pitcher, you're going to have a big inning set up. So what we try to do more than anything else is try to read how good the guy at the plate handles the bat and how much speed is on the bases against you.

JOE BUCK: **Tony, if you were in the other dugout managing against Mark McGwire, would you overshift the infield or move an infielder to the outfield like some teams do?**

TONY LA RUSSA: This is a tough one to answer because you certainly don't want to give the other side any help. I've watched Mark more than most of the other guys, and I think you can pick up a little edge if you defend him properly. So I probably am not going to talk about Mark McGwire, because our idea here is to give Mark more hits, not less hits. However, I think that the shift generally is something that you put on a player when your charts show that, when he puts the ball in play, the great, great majority of his hits are in a certain area, like the pull side. You see that quite a bit. If the guy's a dead pull hitter, I think it makes a lot of sense to shift your infield. Let the hitter see it. Maybe he'll adjust his swing and take a ball the other way. This is a common adjustment that you do when there's nobody on, or when there's a runner on first. However, if the guy's in scoring position, then maybe you want to shift your second baseman back over to the other side a little bit so he doesn't — if he's a smart hitter — just punch a little ground ball to second base and cost you a run. I think the shift is there and there are a lot of hitters that are such dead pull hitters that it would make them think twice about their normal swing.

DEFENSE

JOE BUCK: Tony, how do you defend against the squeeze play and do you try to hide the fact that you're ready for it?

TONY LA RUSSA: I don't know if you can be ready for it unless you've stolen the other side's signs. There's no way to be ready for it. The squeeze play has to be communicated first to the hitter and then the easy one is to the runner at third base. The third base coach just walks over and whispers in his ear. As far as whether you're ready for it, at the particular time that you think the squeeze is on, there are two things that you can do. One is to pitchout if you really smell it or if you steal the sign. The other thing is, which is probably more common, the timing to the runner's break from third base. If he breaks too early, the pitcher can see it because he's in his stretch. As he gets ready to make his delivery, if the runner has broken too quickly, then you have an issue of where you throw the ball so that the bunter can't lay it down. Some people would tell you that you throw the ball right at the hitter. If you're a right-handed pitcher throwing at a right-handed hitter, you throw the ball right at the hitter. In other words, make him duck, and the catcher will catch the ball as the runner's tagging on that side of the plate. Other clubs, and I think our club, will chase the ball away from the hitter and then come over and make the tag.

JOE BUCK: Tony, in a hit-and-run situation, who covers second base, the shortstop or the second baseman, or does it vary?

TONY LA RUSSA: It definitely varies, and this is one of those situations where experience in the middle of your infield is very important. What you ask your infielder to do is to understand the type of hitter at bat. For example, you would think the normal tendency with a right-handed hitter is for the second baseman to cover. Vice versa, with a left-handed hitter, the shortstop covers. However, if you know the hitter and you know he's the type of player that sprays the ball, then you may want to mix it up because the hitter may anticipate the second baseman covering if he's right-handed and he'll shoot the ball through the other side. I think what we like to do is give our players a feel for what kind of hitter

DEFENSE

he is. If he's an opposite field hitter and right-handed hitter, then your shortstop wants to cover. You might also look at the pitch that's called, because many times you can tell where the type of pitch will put the ball in play. If it's a right-handed hitter and you see a sinker being thrown in on him — if he swings at that ball, the ball's going to be pulled to the left-hand side, so your second baseman would cover. If it's a slider low and away, then maybe you want your second baseman to stay home and your shortstop cover. So you put all that together, type of hitter, type of pitch, and you make a decision, but you should vary it.

JOE BUCK: Tony, when the eighth place hitter is up with two outs and the bases empty, why doesn't the outfield play shallower?

TONY LA RUSSA: Now that's a good question. If there is nobody on base, I think the answer is, who is the eighth place hitter? The way the question is set up leads you to believe that they're talking about a line drive type that has occasional power. I think it's a very good point, because when you're defending the outfield, what you try to do, as long as the scoreboard allows you, is take away the ball that's going to be hit the most often. If you think about it, that's a line drive, a blooper or a routine fly ball. For all of those, the more shallow you play, you catch the blooper, you catch the line drive, and you get back on the routine fly ball. The deeper you play, the less you can handle the ball that's hit the most often. So, I think it's a great point. The one thing that you look into sometimes is, some outfielders get very uncomfortable if they play too shallow. I'll give you a great example. About the only thing that you could point at, or scratch your head at with Willie McGee is that he hated to play shallow in the outfield. If it's a question of a making a guy uncomfortable, where he may not catch the ball, then you take a pass on that. But I don't think it's a bad idea at all.

DEFENSE

JOE BUCK: **Tony, how do you determine who plays which spot in the outfield? What are you looking for in a left fielder, center fielder, and right fielder?**

TONY LA RUSSA: If you're building the perfect ball club, what you would try to do is have a right-handed thrower in left field and a left-handed thrower in right field. Also, you like to have a center fielder that has great range and has a very strong throwing arm. Normally, people look at the corner spots, and they would say if a guy doesn't throw as well put him in left field, the better arm goes to right field , and there's something to that. One of the biggest plays in baseball offensively against you is a runner on first base, a base hit to right field, and the runner keeps going around. That's first and third with one out, and they're probably going to score a run against you. If you have a very good arm in right field, that runner will hesitate before he tries to take that extra base. What I look at is the strength of the arms and how much range and mobility they have. I'll tell you one thing that I think is kind of cute. Outfields in different parks are different. There are sometimes when right field is the big part with a lot of range. Sometimes it's left field. So, if you have a very mobile corner guy, sometimes it makes sense to switch, like a J.D. Drew and a Bobby Bonilla. You play J.D. on the big side of the field and Bobby on the smaller one. It's really nice for the Cardinals because we have three center fielders playing our outfield with Ray, Jim, and J.D. They could play anywhere.

PITCHING

JOE BUCK: Tony, when they say a pitcher has "good stuff," are they referring to the ball movement or velocity, or are they referring to how well the pitcher is hitting the catcher's target?

TONY LA RUSSA: "Good stuff" always means the type of speed and movement of a pitcher, referring to his velocity or movement. It does not refer to a location. Often scouts will research young pitchers, and they'll be really turned on when they talk about somebody's "good stuff." A lot of your high draft choices are players with lively arms —their velocity is in the 90s. They have biting, breaking balls. That stuff is very exciting, because the potential is, when you add location, it's going to be very difficult to hit. What you'll find in the big leagues, there's as many guys who are pitching successfully in the big leagues that don't have very terrific "stuff," but really have terrific location. In fact, if you wanted to pick a big league pitcher that's going to be successful, and you had to sacrifice one or the other, location is the thing that gets outs. "Good stuff" that's not well located does not very often get you enough outs over the course of a game. Obviously, when you have someone who has really good stuff and really good location, such as a guy like Roger Clemens or Randy Johnson, then you're talking about the premier guys that nobody hits.

JOE BUCK: Is it ever a good idea for a pitcher with an 0-2 count to not waste a pitch and instead go right after the hitter, go right after the out?

TONY LA RUSSA: This is one of the areas Dave Duncan has been so remarkable. For years there was the idea that the 0-2 pitch could no way be put in play for a base hit, and that paralyzed pitchers so much that the 0-2 pitch was exactly what it's called - a waste pitch. When you only have so many pitches to retire a hitter, why would you want to waste any of them? If you have a guy at 0-2, the most important thing you realize is that he's at the biggest disadvantage he'll be in during the entire time at bat. You can't have a guy at a greater disadvantage than 0-2. Instead of doing the guy a favor by wasting a pitch that gives him even one

PITCHING

ball and starts to give him a little feel that he might be able to save the at bat, you want to try to bury the hitter right then and there. Normally, it involves having an idea what the strikeout pitch is. That involves the hitter and the type of pitcher. It may be that the guy has a killer curve ball, maybe he has a killer forkball, or maybe he has a fastball he throws by guys. However, the 0-2 count is something to remember, because the hitters are very vulnerable. You should go for the pitch. It gives you the best chance to get them out, including a strikeout on that very pitch. Do not waste any pitches.

JOE BUCK: Okay Tony La Russa, here's today's question. An important makeup double header is coming up. You're pitching your hottest starter and one who's been struggling lately, and both are well rested. Which pitcher starts the first game?

TONY LA RUSSA: That's one of the great questions that baseball fans can get into. I think that's one of the beauties of this game. You can receive so many different opinions and they can all be good opinions because, who's to say which one is right or wrong? I've seen outstanding managers go both ways. Some guys say, "Hey, I'm going to take my hot guy; I want to win Game 1". Then you do the best that you can for Game 2, so you'll expend the whole bullpen, you know what you've got left, and you don't have to save anybody. The other one says, "Hey, I like the idea that the first game of a doubleheader is usually a kind of an even-steven game. I pick up a psychological edge if our club and their club knows I've got the big horse waiting for Game 2." You've played the first game, you know what you have to expend, and you can push the hot guy farther. I think you look at who you're pitching against, so you may decide there's a better match up as far as your starting pitcher against their combination of starters. I've seen it go both ways. I don't think there's a correct answer to that question.

PITCHING

JOE BUCK: Okay Tony La Russa, here's today's question. Explain the difference between the setup man's role and the role of your closer.

TONY LA RUSSA: I think that's just one of the questions people are going to say that's an easy one to answer, but I'm going to make a point about the importance of both jobs. Obviously, the setup man is exactly as it sounds when you explain it. You're setting up the last three, four, five, or six outs for the guy you consider to be your closer, and most ball clubs build their bullpen around a closer, and other players close when he's tired or not available. So, the difference is: A closer is a guy that closes the game out for your team. He's the last guy that's going to pitch, and the guy that's going to get the statistic "save." Lately, they've been using the "hold" just to recognize the point I wanted to make. For example, you're playing a ball game and you have a one-run lead going into the seventh inning. The last nine outs you get — three in the seventh, three in the eight, three in the ninth — all of those outs in all of those innings are very important, and the setup guy is just as important as your closer. He really doesn't receive the kind of recognition and the statistics that the closer does. However, I'll tell you on our ball club — on any ball club — we always treat our setup guys like stars just like you do with your closer. Because if he is not effective, you never get to the closer, you don't have the lead, you blow the lead, and there goes the game.

JOE BUCK: Tony, how do you determine whether a pitcher is better suited for a starting pitching role or coming out of the bullpen?

TONY LA RUSSA: I think the number of pitches in his repertoire is probably the best indication. You cannot be a good starting pitcher if you're limited to a couple of pitches that are true out pitches in the major leagues, unless those out pitches are remarkable. For example: Randy Johnson has a dominating fastball and dominating slider. He doesn't really bother with a change-up

PITCHING

much. However, most guys will just have either average or good fastballs and breaking balls. If a hitter only has to face two pitches, and he has several at bats in a game to face them, he'll eliminate one of the two pitches and he'll get on the other. So, what you look for is the number of pitches. Generally, a starting pitcher has to have at least three pitches he can throw for strikes in crucial situations. Four would be even better, since that gives him another option. The relief pitcher usually has to have one dominating pitch he can go to in a key situation. You're always looking at a fewer number of outs, so he can go with one pitch, like Bruce Sutter's forkball or Dennis Eckersley's great command of his fastball. Two is what you usually get from a reliever, and it's anything more than two, then you think about a starting pitcher.

JOE BUCK: Okay Tony La Russa, here's today's question. In addition to stamina, what attributes must a starting pitcher have in order to be consistently effective?

TONY LA RUSSA: I think the number of major league quality pitches he commands is an important part of being a successful pitcher. That's why sometimes you'll take a pitcher and make him a reliever. For example, he has two very good major league pitches — that's more like a reliever, because if you go as a starter, a hitter will just subtract one of the two. If you have a fastball and a curve ball and you really have nothing else to complement that — as a starter you're going to have to go through the lineup three or four times, then the good hitters can just take one of the pitches away from you. They'll just think, "I'm not going to swing at a curve ball. I'll just swing at his fastball." So a starter has to have at least three pitches. If he has four pitches, then he should have a lot of weapons so he can go after a hitter using a couple of them, and he can change what his out pitch is later on. I think the number of pitches that you command that are of major league quality is really an important quality for a pitcher. Now, a quick comment on stamina. What you really want to watch is how much your starter pitcher is laboring, because his stamina will be affected. He may be more tired after throwing 60 pitches where he's out of whack

PITCHING

than 120 where he's in a good groove and there's much less stress on his arm.

JOE BUCK: **Tony, what characteristic does a pitcher need to be an effective closer?**

TONY LA RUSSA: He's got to have a certain killer mentality. In other words, there's something to taking the mound in the ninth inning to get three outs, and you know those three outs end it. You also know as you walk out there, the club has played for eight innings to get that lead. That means the starting pitcher and whatever other relievers have done a certain job; the defense and the offense have done a certain job. There's a lot invested in one single game where you've got the lead. To me, one of the most fascinating developments in baseball is that, as the closer takes the mound, he's aware of all this. You have to have a certain strength, or mental, internal fortitude. I start with the player that has the guts to be a closer because there is something to getting those last three outs. You need to be able to throw the ball fairly often. You just can't be available once or twice a week. But when it comes to getting those three outs, you have to have some type of dominating pitch or pitches that make it very difficult for the other side, because everybody's keyed up to get those last three outs.

JOE BUCK: **Okay Tony La Russa, here's today's question. Premier closers possess a unique combination of patience and tenacity. Describe the art of finishing a ballgame.**

TONY LA RUSSA: It's a very important job — to me it's my favorite player on a team. The reason is because he's the only player on the ball club who, if he has a great day, your team is sure to win. Nobody else can: You may have a pitcher who pitches nine innings and gives up one unearned run, and you may lose 1-0. The great closers that I've seen are very competitive, and I think that's the big thing that comes out. They know the game is on the line, and they really get into the competition. I've had the pleasure of watching Dennis Eckersley for 10 years. He's always ready to

PITCHING

pitch. He always understands the game is on his shoulders, and he just gets ready with fear. His fear is that the team has worked for eight innings to get the lead, and he can mess it all up in one inning. So his fear really puts him on edge, and he tries his best all of the time. I think competitiveness is very important, and you have to have a lot of courage in a very tough situation, because if players are on base and a base hit beats you, then it's all wasted. You have to really have guts for that type of role.

JOE BUCK: Now Tony La Russa, here's today baseball question. Tony, it wasn't that long ago that starting pitchers regularly worked on three days rest, but now that only seems to happen in the post season if at all. What brought about this change?

TONY LA RUSSA: This is one of those questions we discuss every year, and it's discussed all across baseball. I think a big part of the answer is conditioning. Years ago pitchers were conditioned, from the time they signed a professional contract to the time they came to the big leagues, to work with three days rest. However, for a long time, as long as I've been around, the pattern is to give pitchers four days of rest between their starts. What you find now with pitchers, if you had to try to shorten their pitching rest by one day, you would run the risk of two things. Number one, you'd run the risk of hurting their arm because they're just not conditioned to do that. Secondly, the quality of their stuff usually suffers. One of the points you need to make here is the type of pitcher. With the Cardinals, for example, most of our guys have some power to their pitching. That extra day of rest allows them to get that little extra on their fastball. You give them a day short in rest, and they usually lose some velocity of the fastball. It's usually good for a sinkerball pitcher who relies on movement and control.

PITCHING

JOE BUCK: Now Tony La Russa, here's today baseball question. With expansion coming again and all the talk about lack of quality pitching, should teams consider going back to a four-man rotation? Or what about a system in which you team up starters and relievers so that each goes more often, but for fewer innings at a time?

TONY LA RUSSA: Here again, this is a great question that's debated almost without end every year. One of the things to think about is a four-man rotation, and the fans toss it up, they talk about this a lot. One of the practical problems is that you need four players who can pitch with three days rest. On one of the earlier shows, we talked about power type guys usually suffering if they have to go out there every fourth day. They usually don't have that velocity, and you run the risk of injury. If you have four guys who rely on movement and location more than they rely on stuff, then you can get away with it. You would have to mold your rotation around four players who can do it. One guy who can't screws up the whole deal. The other thing is: There has been a three-man rotation. We did that in Oakland one year, just as an experiment, where you have three players whom you start every third day, and the rest of your bullpen complements them. It really is a fascinating theory. I think that if you had an expansion club and you wanted to set up your pitching staff, you'd have to set up your relievers to complement those three starters. You could present a lot of problems. But here again, breaking tradition is a very difficult thing to do.

JOE BUCK: Why do some relief pitchers often choose to pitch from the stretch even when the bases are empty?

TONY LA RUSSA: This is something we didn't see for a long time and then lately — I don't know what lately means, but maybe a few years ago — a few players did it, and now almost all of them do it. The common sense explanation they will give and the pitching coaches will give is that a reliever generally will come into a situation in the middle of an inning with runners on base. He'll work

PITCHING

in the bullpen from the stretch and eliminate one part of getting ready in the bullpen. If he has to get his warm ups ready from the stretch position and the windup position, he's doubling his preparation. Normally, you'll have a short time span, so you want to reduce the preparation time and not have more things to worry about. I think what you'll see from most pitchers is that they like to work from the stretch because it's one less thing to get ready, and the other thing, which is kind of cute, is that most pitchers' deliveries from the stretch are technically and fundamentally more sound. There are more ways for a windup to go wrong than from a stretch. Not only are you simplifying what you do to get ready, it technically gets you in better shape mechanically.

JOE BUCK: Some pitchers don't throw the ball as hard as others but have good control. Is there a minimum velocity a major league pitcher has to have in his fastball to survive, even if he has great control?

TONY LA RUSSA: There's a couple ways to look at this question. For example, Tom Seaver, who is the smartest pitcher that I've ever seen on a ball club as a manager, would say velocity is the least of the pitcher's assets when it comes to helping win a game. It's much more location and movement. There are a lot of pitchers who don't have blazing fastballs, but if they have the ability to throw the ball where they want with some type of movement, that's what is needed. One important asset: If their fastball has movement, and they're able to bend it in some way with a slider or breaking ball. Another very big asset is being able to change speeds with the same-looking arm movement. So if you can throw 85, which is just an average fastball, and with the same motion throw an 80 or 70 mile an hour change-up, that deception will keep the hitter off-balance, and you can be successful in the big leagues. The important part of this question is the minimum speed. If your maximum speed is only 80 miles an hour, then there will not be a enough difference between your change of speed and your best fastball, so hitters will be in one zone and you can not be successful.

PITCHING

JOE BUCK: How should a pitcher throw to a hitter he's never faced before?

TONY LA RUSSA: In part, I think it's the same way he would throw to a hitter he has seen before. The best answer, I believe, is that a pitcher pitches to his strength. You see more problems in the big leagues with pitchers getting bogged down with scouting reports. They'll say this guy is a high fastball hitter, so now he tries to throw sinkers or he tries to throw breaking balls when he's a high fastball pitcher. What you try to do more than anything else is teach the pitcher a style that deals with his strengths, and then you throw those strengths against the hitter. With that being said, when you scout a young hitter or a new hitter, if you watch and you've been around for a little bit, you'll see if the guy has a pull tendency or whether he uses the entire field. If he has a pull tendency, normally you want to do something in off the plate to set up and to get him out of the way. If he's a player that sprays the ball, then you probably want to make sure you throw the ball in enough for strikes, because he is looking out over the plate more. It depends on the type of hitter, and you make the adjustment whether you think he's up strong or down strong. More than anything else, you want your pitchers throwing to their strength. Don't get too bogged down on the type of hitter.

JOE BUCK: Before the start of a series what types of things do you tell your pitchers about the other teams hitters?

TONY LA RUSSA: I think this is one area where you have to be careful. You can bog your pitchers down with too much information about what other hitters do. You always want to remind them that it's important to pitch to their strength. For example, T.J. Matthews has certain strengths. His strengths are different from Mark Petkovsek, who is different from Dennis Eckersley. You want to give them some general information about the hitters, but you don't want to paralyze them with information to where a player who is a good fastball pitcher is afraid to throw his fastball, because he is thinking, "Oh, this guy is just a deadly

PITCHING

fastball type hitter." Tell your pitchers which hitters are more prone to swing early in the count. Tell them where they can go on the plate to get an early strike. You might want to tell them what type of power, where their power area is, and where they're vulnerable. For example, this player chases breaking balls if you get them down and out of the strike zone. If you leave a breaking ball in the strike zone, that's one of his power pitches. So you give him information that's helpful, but you don't want to scare him or get him off his style.

JOE BUCK: Do you normally place pitchers on pitch counts or limit the innings they pitch or does it differ from pitcher to pitcher?

TONY LA RUSSA: Normally, the reason you look at pitch count, and it's not because of some hard and fast rule, is you start to learn when a certain pitcher fatigues. It may be something early in the season and you're being careful to get players in the best of shape. It may be some players — and this is typically true — have a certain range of pitches, and beyond that they'll start to become vulnerable to getting hit or getting hurt. Depending on how strong they are, it differs with pitchers. What you do in a particular game is: You factor in how that game is going. For example, sometimes a pitcher is throwing in such great rhythm and in such a good routine, that if he's normally getting tired at 110, and he's had such a good game it's been almost effortless, then you can give him 120. Sometimes that same pitcher has been laboring so much that when he gets to 90, he's out of gas because it's been such an effort that day. So, pitch count is just one of the things you look at. But you will start to learn with pitch counts that there is a danger area for all of these players, and it differs on the type of strength and type of delivery they have.

PITCHING

JOE BUCK: **How many types of pitches does a starter need to have in order to be a successful pitcher in the big leagues?**

TONY LA RUSSA: I'll give you the general rule. I think most people agree if you have three quality major league pitches, you can definitely be a success in the major leagues. I think it's possible to pitch successfully if you have two, but if you have more than three, you could be very successful. However, a word of caution: It's tough to have four quality pitches. What usually happens is that the fourth pitch not only doesn't become very effective, but it tends to take something away from the other three. So what you look for is, obviously, a good fastball, one of the breaking balls, and a real quality change-up or forkball. That's usually your basic requirement to be a successful starting pitcher. As a starter you need to face the lineup two, three, or four times, and you just can't come out with a limited number of weapons. If you're coming out with just a fastball and breaking ball, what hitters will do is subtract one of those and just look for the other. So you need to have at least three pitches, and if you can show them one time through it, then the next time you give something else, a third time you give something else. You need to have that kind of arsenal.

JOE BUCK: **Tony, are there any indicators that a pitcher is not throwing well during the course of the game?**

TONY LA RUSSA: The best one is when there are a lot of guys on base and a lot of runs being scored. The trick, I think, when you handle pitching is to try to see to evaluate how the pitcher is doing before the damage. I think it's the classic things that you look for, once you get to know the pitcher — I don't want to go by that too quickly, because it's very important to get to know your pitcher. You will start to recognize his keys, and you'll see the groove he gets into, his arm angle, his point of release, and you start to see when he has his good fastball and you'll see what kind of action it has. Usually, guys have a strong side of the plate, so you'll see how effective he is getting the ball there. You'll see what kind of breaking pitches he has when he's right, so once you have that

PITCHING

baseline information, then you watch the game that day and you see how his stuff compares to his normal. The classic things that you look for: If you start to see a guy get a fastball up in the strike zone, that's usually bad. If you see breaking pitches that are rolling and not snapping, that's usually an indication he doesn't have his good stuff. I'll tell you another one we look for is arm speed. When you see the guy's arm speed really back off, that's a good sign of fatigue.

JOE BUCK: Tony, you hear people say that more pitchers should challenge hitters with their fastball. Is that always a good strategy?

TONY LA RUSSA: That's like most things you say quickly and you try to have a quick or easy answer, you get into trouble. I think there's a point you can see a pitcher be too tentative or not aggressive enough. He doesn't trust his stuff and you're thinking, "Man I just wish he would come after hitters more." Usually, the fastball is the most effective pitch. You have your best chance to control it, and it's still the most difficult pitch to hit. Also, a breaking ball not thrown well can be hit farther and longer. I think when we talk to our pitchers about being aggressive, we talk to them about being aggressive with all their pitches. I think sometimes a pitcher will fall into that trap when you say, "You're not being aggressive enough, you're being too tentative." So he wants to throw a fastball right down the middle. You do that to a major league hitter. and you're going to give up big damage. We try to talk about aggressive, but being aggressive with all of their pitches. I don't just think that it has to be a fastball. A good breaking ball in a key situation is an aggressive stance and aggressive attitude. Aggressiveness has to be matched to the pitcher and the situation, not always with the fastball.

PITCHING

JOE BUCK: Tony, with so many hitters leaning over the plate these days and some even wearing pads to do it, why don't more pitchers take command and throw the ball inside?

TONY LA RUSSA: That's a great question. That's a perennial problem year in and year out. It raises the issue: If you're throwing the ball inside, you're just pitching inside as part of the game, but if they throw inside, you think they're trying to hit you. It causes a lot of friction in a lot of games you see. Throwing inside is, undoubtedly, one of the biggest keys to being a successful pitcher. When you see a hitter who's really on top of the plate, you probably get more upset when you see all the padding the wears than anything, such as a guy like Craig Biggio, for example, or Barry Bonds. They have these huge pads they wear on their arms and they lean over the plate. They dare you to throw inside. In fact Biggio very often will lean into the pitch. So it's a little bit dangerous to throw inside, because you might hit them and that means a base runner. One tactic that we use a lot is, because pitching inside is so very important, we try to throw the ball down and in. If the pitch is up and in, guys turn into it. They take it on their pad or on their back, it doesn't sting, and you lose a base. If you throw it down and in, hitters will always move their feet, and no hitter likes to be unstable at the plate where he's not sure about his footing. So we like down and in better than at his elbow or back.

JOE BUCK: Tony, a quick and easy question. Why is it so important for a pitcher to get ahead of the hitter?

TONY LA RUSSA: There are all kinds of ways to make this point to your pitchers. You can look at the batting average of hitters. For example, the count is 0-0 where they're even, and then it becomes 1-0, 2-0, 2-1, and 3-1. You look at the average for hitters, and if it's a guy that's a respectable-to-good hitter, his batting average keeps jumping and jumping, to where if you are a good hitter, you're hitting .400 when you've really got the count in your favor. Why? Because the more the count goes in your favor, the more the

PITCHING

pitcher has to throw a strike and has to use more of the plate to get the ball over the plate. When he's ahead at the plate, most good hitters will zone the particular pitcher. They'll look for a ball in an area where they can really juice it. If the ball is not in that area, then they'll just take it and they'll have a pitch, a strike or two, to play with. So one of the key things is, you just reverse it. If you get strike one, you immediately put the hitter on the defensive. Make him enlarge a strike zone, rather than narrow it, and all of a sudden now you may have him chasing the ball in the corner, or chasing the ball up or down. Any time you get a hitter swinging out of the happy area, you're going to get the ball off the fat part of the bat.

JOE BUCK: Tony, what real difference does it make if you start a right-handed pitcher or a left-hander? Most teams do not have an entire right-handed or left-handed hitting lineup, so the starter will have to face both types of hitters anyway.

TONY LA RUSSA: The best answer is you want to pick your best pitcher whether he's right-handed or left-handed. If you had players that were absolutely even and you wanted to make a choice, a lot of guys would figure the left-handed starter would be better. They have an advantage nullifying the other club's running game, if they have any kind of move. Most lineups are set up against the majority of pitchers, which are right-handed, so if they have some key left-handed hitters, then a left-handed starter will help nullify a left-handed hitter. They may even get up and get him out of the lineup. The other thing is that right-handed hitters face right-handed pitchers all the time, so they're not as affected by the percentage move. I've seen clubs win that have all right-handed hitters. You don't see a club that has all left-handed hitters win very often, because that left-handed starter can dominate them so easily. The best solution for a rotation is to have right-handers and left-handers, because balance and variety create more problems for the other club's offense. I guess if I had to pick a perfect rotation, I'd have three left-handers and two right-handers in it.

PITCHING

JOE BUCK: Tony, ideally, how often can you use your primary closer without over-using his arm?

TONY LA RUSSA: The only way to answer that question is to track it day by day. What was true in April may not be true in June. What's true in June may not be true in September. It's really a day-to-day situation, and the healthiest situation is one where you have total honesty and where the closer understands how important he is. In fact, a lot of managers will say their closer is their favorite player, because he's the only guy that can guarantee a win. If he has a great day, you'll win the game. Nobody else can guarantee that, not even a starter who pitches a shutout. You may not score a run, and it would be tied at zero. What you want to do is to have your closer come in every day, talk to the pitching coach, talk to the trainer, and talk to the manager, especially when — in this situation where you're talking about over-use — this means you've been using him quite a bit. Let him tell you honestly how he feels. What you'll find out sometimes is, because he's in a good groove with good mechanics, that even though he's been pitching a lot, he hasn't been fatiguing his arm. There may be other times where he's really struggling and you've pitched him only a couple times in a week, but he's actually more tired and stiff, because he's out of whack. So you really need to communicate, and the key is: You always want to err on the side of caution.

JOE BUCK: Tony, what qualities make a pitcher a good spot starter?

TONY LA RUSSA: That's one of those unique ones. Not a lot of guys can do this, because normally by spot starter it means he's spending a lot of time in the bullpen. The normal reliever is a guy who probably has a limited arsenal. You're talking about a player with two or maybe three pitches, probably two, and he can throw often. A spot starter is somebody that really needs to have more than two. The guy that has the versatility to pitch well out of the bullpen and accept a spot start, has to be somebody with more than two pitches who has some durability, endurance and stamina

PITCHING

to his arm so that he can give you more than a couple of innings. A lot of your relievers are conditioned to just throw somewhere between fifteen and thirty pitches. That's why it's so important on a pitching staff, as you put it together, to have innings guys in your bullpen. In other words, note that spot starter, the emergency guy you can go to, who's got some stamina. I think the criteria would be stamina to pitch more than 30 pitches. He needs to get up there to 50, 70, or 100 pitches and also more than two types of pitches.

JOE BUCK: **Tony, a double play is sometimes referred to as a pitcher's best friend. Are there things a pitcher can do to help get a hitter to ground into a double play?**

TONY LA RUSSA: Absolutely. The number one thing is getting the ball down with some movement on it. If you're looking for a double play, and you get the ball up, such as waist and above, every once in a while the hitter will top hand that thing and chop it, and you'll get away with it. However, most of the time pitchers that have thrown waist and above, if they're put in play and they are put in play in the air, there goes your double play chance. What you try to do is get the ball down with movement. Normally, if you can get the ball to the corners, that's the second key to this situation. If it's a right-handed hitter, you want to get the ball down and in. They'll pull the ball to the third baseman. Or down and away, so they won't be able to center it. It's the same thing for a left-handed hitter. It's not enough, by the way, to just try to get the ball down, because if it's down over the middle, a lot of hitters can just drop the bat head on that, and they'll hit a nice line drive or maybe hit the ball out of the park. It's really getting the ball down and moving it to the edges — in or out.

PITCHING

JOE BUCK: Tony, is there anything a manager or pitching coach can do to lessen the number of walks a team gives up? Are walks more mental than physical?

TONY LA RUSSA: Yes, there are several things you can do. For one, you can put pitchers on your staff who throw strikes. You can take the pitchers that are very erratic and send them someplace else. In today's baseball, pitching is pretty limited as far as alternatives, so what you would like to do and what you have to do don't always go together. As far as other things that you can do to help, you can emphasize — and I think we emphasize it as much as anybody — that successful pitching in the big leagues starts with strike one. It's much better to throw strike one to the hitter at the plate and then take your chances he might take that first strike and hit it for a base hit. However, that's strike one, so if he doesn't connect safely, that will really put you in charge of the count We really encourage that philosophy. We encourage the fact that aggressiveness wins in the big leagues. Putting a lot of runners on base, you're going to get burned sooner or later. I think you have to back up that theory with not pitching players in situations who haven't shown command if you have an alternative in another direction.

JOE BUCK: Tony, what sort of a limit do you place on your closer's workload? Is it a certain number of pitches per appearance, or a number of appearances in a row, or is it something else?

TONY LA RUSSA: This is a great question, and it's really flexible. A lot of it is just common sense. You have to read your closers, and they vary. Some pitchers have the true rubber arm and can throw very often. Some are more max-effort types. When they're done pitching, if it's a legitimate save situation where they had to work hard to get three outs, they'll have some extra stiffness, or maybe some soreness. You have to read your pitcher to see how quickly he bounces back. Once you've got that, then you start looking at the games. You have to remember it's a six-month season. You

PITCHING

need to win games early, middle, and late, and if you get into the post-season, you still want the closer to have something left. The general rule: If you can pitch your guy a couple of days in a row, that's okay, but three is really pushing it. Don't do three too often. If he does three, then you've got to give him a couple of days off. That's why it's so important to have some protection for your closer with other players on the staff who can also pitch the ninth inning. I think the thing you most want to watch is his delivery. If he's throwing the ball easy, pitches don't pile up on him. If he's struggling, four or five can really break him.

JOE BUCK: **Tony, explain what makes a pitcher a ground ball pitcher as opposed to a fly ball pitcher.**

TONY LA RUSSA: It probably has to do with two factors more than anything else: movement and location. By movement, if the ball has got some running or sinking action, then you're going to be a ground ball pitcher, as long as running and sinking is at the lower part of the strike zone. If you've got some extra velocity and your ball has a little hop, if your fastball's got a little hop as it gets near the plate, you're going to be a fly ball pitcher if you get that up in the strike zone. If you try to throw that same hopping fastball low, hitters can drop the head on it and you won't have as much success. Another way to look at it is — just look at one of our pitchers on the 2000 Cardinals who has the versatility to do both, and that's our closer Dave Veres. Dave Veres, when he gets his fastball down in the strike zone, you'll see that running action and he'll get ground balls. If he throws the ball above the waist, when he has his normal velocity, the ball will have a little hop to it and you'll see him get some fly balls. So it's really up and down, movement and location that factor into what makes a pitcher a ground ball pitcher.

PITCHING

JOE BUCK: Tony, when a pitcher is constantly slow between each pitch, what impact can that have on the hitter and what about the impact on his own defense?

TONY LA RUSSA: It's probably one of the things pitchers can control easily that would make them so much better. If you think about the effect on fans, there is nothing worse than having to sit a long time between pitches. However, if you think about your defense, they're on their toes if you work with a good tempo. It's the opposite if you're taking too much time between pitches. Think about the hitter. If you're the pitcher, the message you're sending in between each pitch, if you're just taking a lot of time, is you're letting him know you're unsure and you're not confident. A pitcher who works quickly gives exactly the opposite message with, "Hey, I'm coming after you. I know exactly what I want to do. I know I can get you." Hitters do not like pitchers that work quickly. Hitters have more to think about in between pitches than pitchers do, so a pitcher who works quickly kind of disrupts their preparation, because the count changes and they may want to say, I'm 1 and 0 versus 0 and 1. The pitcher who's working quickly really disrupts their tempo. Working quickly is one of the best things a pitcher can do. You only want to fall back on slowing up when you're occasionally having a problem pulling it all together.

JOE BUCK: Tony, teams seem to keep the ball away from Mark McGwire but come inside more on Sammy Sosa. How do you pitch to power hitters like McGwire, Sosa, Bagwell and Griffey?

TONY LA RUSSA: They're each different enough so that one way against them all is not the right way. Each player has his own unique style. One thing that really marks a Bagwell and a Griffey, for example, is they're usually hitting in the .300s. As you know, Mark's average has been high the last several years — you know, right at .300. Sosa has elevated his average where he's now a .300 hitter. What that tells you is that these guys are making adjustments at the plate. I think the best answer to this question

PITCHING

is: You may have an idea how you're going after them, but as soon as you establish that pattern, these guys will make an adjustment, and they'll get to that pitch. If you want to pitch Sosa inside, he'll look inside and hammer you. You'd have to go away, and then he would make the adjustment away. You'd have to come back inside or go back and forth. All these good hitters are terrific at adjusting, and that's a part of being successful in the big leagues, with no obvious holes, and I think that's true for all these guys. It's not just tjat they have power, but they're very good hitters.

JOE BUCK: Tony, with so many smaller ballparks being built, are pitchers being taught to pitch in a different way than they used to?

TONY LA RUSSA: Absolutely! Even in the old days you would have small ballparks — Fenway Park is a good example in the American League. What you try to do in Fenway Park is now what you do in a lot of ballparks that are small. By that I mean, if a ballpark's small, most of the time anything out over the plate has a chance to go out of the park. What you try to teach in a small ballpark is: You need to be aggressive, and you need to pitch inside a lot because you don't want that extension where anything in the air will leave the park. We talk pitching "in" enough to where the hitter doesn't lean out and has a lot of plate coverage. You need to try to challenge players and be aggressive. This is because, in a small ballpark, the more players earn a base on balls — you know if you're thinking small, be careful ... ball one, ball four; then you walk a couple of guys, you get a ball out over the plate, and it's a three-run homer. You're much better off throwing a ball right down the middle and having players hit solo home runs than you are trying to pick. So we think aggressive, go after hitters, get ahead of the counts, and make them a little bit more likely to chase and get the ball inside where they can't extend.

PITCHING

JOE BUCK: Tony, how many different pitches does a pitcher need to be effective at the major league level?

TONY LA RUSSA: This is a comprehensive question and there are several answers. It really depends on the role you have. I think the classic way to look at it, as a reliever, if you have one dominant pitch, then you can be a true short reliever. If you're going to get more than one, two, or three outs as a reliever, then you're going to need at least two quality pitches. If you're a starting pitcher, you better have at least three quality pitches if you expect to go through the lineup three or four times. If you have two dominant pitches and one that's pretty good, then you're still going to be a good starter, because you'll give the hitters enough to worry about. I think a good part of this answer, an interesting part to this answer, would be the possibility that one pitch can be more than one pitch. By that I mean, take your fastball — if you use a two-seam fastball and a four-seam fastball, you actually have two fastballs. If you use both, if you use a two-seam fastball down in the zone, in and out, and you use a four-seam fastball up in the zone, in and out, it's almost like four fastballs. If you take a little bit off a fastball, such as a batting practice fastball, which is harder than a change up, it's like five fastballs. Same as far as a slow curve ball for a strike or a curve ball in the dirt, you can do something with all those pitches. But you need at least two or three.

STATISTICS

JOE BUCK: Okay Tony La Russa, here's today's question. In evaluating a pitcher, are there benchmarks you use such as strikeout-to-walk ratios, hits-to-innings pitched ratios, or strikeouts per nine innings? How much faith do you put in these statistical measurements for a pitcher?

TONY LA RUSSA: I think the answer is that they are helpful, but they're not controlling. That is a very important difference. When you're trying to get a reading on a pitcher, things like a lot of base on balls are dangerous, and that doesn't usually fit good pitching. A lot of strikeouts are not necessarily as great as you would think because strikeouts mean a lot of pitches, and that sometimes means that you'll only go five or six innings. A pitcher who's being more economical and getting the ball put in play will go deeper into the game, which is better for your pitching staff. I think a key stat though, a key ratio, is your hits per innings pitched. I think when a player has fewer hits per innings pitched, it's a good indication he's got the kind of stuff that gives hitters trouble. To me, the stats that are most important are: If you see somebody with a history in the minor leagues of being a winner, even if his ERA is inflated, pay attention to him because that means he's not afraid to win a game. When the game is on the line, he has a knack for making the pitch that gets him the out that gets him in the clubhouse a winner.

JOE BUCK: There are so many statistics in the game of baseball: batting average, on-base average, slugging percentage and so on. What statistics do you look at when you evaluate a hitter?

TONY LA RUSSA: I remember when I went to school I had to take a course called, "The Use and Abuse of Statistics." I think it's something that's a real problem in baseball because so many things are analyzed. In hitting, for example, you can get bogged down with stuff that gets in the way of evaluating a hitter. The way you evaluate a hitter is to watch him swing and watch the ball come off his bat, and you look at his success. Obviously, as far as

STATISTICS

stats, you look at what type of hitter he is and what does he provide to your team? If it's somebody that hits at the top of the lineup, the thing that you're going to look at is on-base percentage — a very big key, and that's got to translate into runs scored. If it's a guy who hits in the middle of the line-up, the number one thing you're looking at is runs produced. Batting average is important, but if you've got a guy who hits .220 and then drives in 110 runs, he's doing one part of his job. One thing you learn, the guy who hits .290 and drives in 95, he's also getting on base and creating opportunities for somebody else. I think it depends on where you want him to hit, but don't get bogged in too many of the very strange stats. Stay with the basics.

JOE BUCK: **Tony, why don't we hear baseball people talk much about statistics like slugging percentage or on-base percentage? Aren't these key indicators of run production?**

TONY LA RUSSA: I think it depends upon your baseball person. In fact, with different baseball people — and that's one of the beauties of baseball — it's a matter of opinion. Some people think that one particular stat is a real indicator of how successful a pitcher or a hitter, here we're talking about hitting, would be. Other people would talk about different stats. In Oakland, for example, Sandy Alderson was a big advocate of on-base percentage. He felt that if you had power and on-base percentage, you would have a successful club. Other people would look at different stats. I do believe that on-base percentage — the number of times you can get guys on base — is a key way to evaluate how successful your club can be, how good a player is, or how productive he'll be for your team. I think the challenge as you put together your offense is to try to put together a blend of speed and power. You don't just want to go for slugging percentage. Your on-base percentage guy, for example, if he's also a stolen base guy, now makes one base equal to two or three. To me, stats fit the situation. You can use them and abuse them.

STATISTICS

JOE BUCK: Tony, you get scouting reports to help evaluate players you haven't seen, but fans only have statistics. Are there any particular stats you think are especially revealing about a hitter?

TONY LA RUSSA: Absolutely, there are stats that can help you evaluate a hitter, whether it's yours or the guy's you're going against. Obviously, the one that gets the most attention nowadays is the match-ups. By that I mean the career success or lack of success that a hitter has against a certain pitcher. There is something that common sense tells you that if Player A gets a lot of hits against Pitcher B, you want to know that. And that tells you something about the hitter or vice versa if he gets no hits. The other type of statistics that you want to know is how often he's putting the ball in play, and a high strikeout total. You want to look at on-base percentage because that shows that you have some type of eye at the plate and have some kind of discipline. You want to look at base-on-balls, since that factors into on-base percentage. Slugging percentage — that's a nice one. That will tell you whether the hitter's got some extra life to his bat or not, or whether he's just an opposite field hitter. I don't know if you call this a hitting stat, but you look at how much base running he does. Those are all things that help you evaluate the type of player he is offensively.

JOE BUCK: Tony, you get scouting reports to help you evaluate players you haven't seen, but fans only have statistics. Are there any particular stats you think are especially revealing about a pitcher?

TONY LA RUSSA: The obvious ones are for a reliever — appearances. You want to know how often he was available to pitch and did pitch, because that tells you two things: If he pitched a lot, it means he was available and the team had confidence and sent him out there. The other thing for a starter is number of starts, because that will tell you durability. Innings pitched — you know the benchmark of 200-plus innings — those are all things that you

STATISTICS

want to know about the starter and the reliever, as far as availability and how often he goes out there. The other thing that you want to look at — one of the best benchmarks — is hits per innings pitched. That's a good one because effective pitchers have a certain ratio that indicates that they're tough for hitters to put the ball in play successfully against. You also want to look at their strikeout ratio; that tells you a lot about the kind of stuff that he has. Is it a player on the other side who puts the ball in play or does he wipe them out? And obviously, does he get the ball over the plate? So walk ratio is another big thing that you want to look at.

MISCELLANEOUS

JOE BUCK: **Okay Tony, here's today's question. In your experience, have you found that a ball will travel better in a dome stadium or an outdoor stadium?**

TONY LA RUSSA: I think if you look at it, the dome stadium is going to be more consistent. The outdoor stadium will depend on wind, temperature and humidity. Is it wind in, wind out, and how cold or warm is it? If you're in an outdoor ballpark where the wind is blowing out, the ball may carry better than in a domed stadium. The ball will carry the same in a dome all the time, so overall the better home run park probably just depends on the dimensions. In Minnesota, it's a very close, small ballpark where you can hit home runs to right, right-center, center, left-center, left. Houston's Astrodome is bigger, so it's tougher to hit home runs. I think that, if the conditions are consistent and ball travel is dependent on fence dimensions, then as far as an outdoor ballpark goes, you just have to check the humidity and wind direction that day. Then you can see whether it's home run possible or it's going to be a tough pitchers day.

JOE BUCK: **Tony, what differences are there in your game strategy when you're playing on grass as opposed to Astroturf?**

TONY LA RUSSA: I think there are definitely considerations. It starts with your lineup. When you know that you're going into a series on turf, you consider the wear and tear that your players face, especially outfielders who are running on that stuff all the time. If anyone is a little ouchy in their legs, the pounding on the turf will make them worse. It will also affect anyone who has a little sore back. We will very often even begin with the lineup and adjust the playing time for the series, the three game series, based on turf versus grass. Then once the game starts, I think you have to be aware that there's a different type game. Bunting on turf is tougher than on grass. Choppers that get by your infielders can turn into two and three bases on turf. You need to position your defense, especially in the outfield, a little differently when you have turf. You have to handle balls in the corner differently if you're an outfielder

MISCELLANEOUS

on turf as opposed to grass. So there are a lot of considerations. I think usually on turf, you may want to lean toward a little more speed. You want to make sure that your infielders playing that day have strong, accurate arms, because they play deeper. There are things to consider, and you hope that you have the flexibility on your roster to be able to do both.

JOE BUCK: Okay Tony, here's today's question. Now that the Cardinals have gone back to a grass field, are they at a disadvantage when they play on an artificial surface, then go back home to grass?

TONY LA RUSSA: No, not really. I think clubs that play on grass have an advantage overall because they will be used to playing on grass. Turf is easier to play on, and the easiest adjustment to make is when you go from grass, like playing at home, to going on the road and playing on turf. The ball is going to bounce truer, and it's an easy adjustment to make. You'll have a tougher adjustment when you finish the turf games, and you go back home to play on grass, but since you've been playing there as your home park, you'll make that adjustment very quickly. I think clubs that play their home games on turf have a tougher time whenever they've got to play on grass on the road.

JOE BUCK: Tony, what qualities do you look for when putting together a coaching staff?

TONY LA RUSSA: I think you start by understanding what a plus a coaching staff can provide a club. If you think about getting together in the middle of February and you're hopefully playing some time around Halloween, that's a lot of time for a team to be together. The players will learn that the coaches can be a tremendous asset or a tremendous negative. What you look for with that group of coaches is expertise, personality and the willingness to work. All those things must be there. For example, it's really good for the players to enjoy the coaching staff. You have

MISCELLANEOUS

some coaches who just have bad personalities; they're negative-type people. The players might understand they have great expertise, a lot to offer, but they get so turned off because the guy's such a jerk or always complaining and so negative that they don't want to listen. The other issue is that you may have terrific personality but nothing to offer. A player comes to you, "Okay, I really want to hear you, man," but the coach opens his mouth and nothing comes out. You really need this combination of personality, expertise and the willingness to work. Working and coaching go together. You can't have a good coach without having that together.

JOE BUCK: Tony, with regard to a hitting instructor, what specific qualities are most important: Someone who has had great success in the big leagues, someone with superior batting technique, or someone with great teaching skills?

TONY LA RUSSA: I think this is probably one of the toughest coaching areas in the major leagues. Being a major league hitting coach is very difficult. If I had to give you a couple of the top qualities, I'd say personality and hard work. Personality, because there's got to be something about the way you connect with your hitters that make them want to believe in you, make them want to work for you, and make them want to please you. Therefore, you might have a lot of really good knowledge about fundamentals, techniques, and maybe even how pitchers are going to pitch against you, but you've got such a blah personality or such a negative personality that the players don't really feed off you. They'll just turn you off and will not respond at all. So I think personality is important. You've got to be willing to work. Mostly 13 or 14 hitters every day need to go out there and get their work done. If you're a lazy type who doesn't like to sweat and get ready to go, you'll not be a good hitting coach. Then you want to add in a good idea of what the fundamentals are and what the mechanics are. You really want to know something about hitting in situations – how you approach the change depends on what you have to do at the plate.

MISCELLANEOUS

JOE BUCK: You and Dave Duncan have worked together for a long time. What makes Dave, a former catcher, such an effective pitching coach?

TONY LA RUSSA: I think the reason that Dave is so outstanding is because he is absolutely complete. You can be a pitcher and be as complete, or as Dave has proven, you can be an ex-catcher. When I say complete, there are a number of things that a pitching coach is supposed to provide to the pitching staff and the catching staff. If you are a pitcher, you wouldn't know as much about the catching side, so you would have to learn it. If you are a catcher, there are certain mechanical things that you have to learn, and Dave has learned them. One reason why Dave is so good is that you can't point out one area where he isn't what we would rate a "10" in that area. What happens is that everyone has different needs, so you may be mechanically strong, and that pitching coach who is strong in that area, he helps that guy. However, another player may need a mental adjustment, and he can't deal with that. Dave handles mental, he also handles mechanical, and he is also a bear for preparation – he really gets into studying the opposition. The pitching coach tries to figure out where the weaknesses are and then adjust the pitcher's style to what the hitter is not supposed to be able to do.

JOE BUCK: Umpires hardly ever change a call, so why do managers run out and even bother to argue?

TONY LA RUSSA: That's one of the most delicate areas in relationships that managers, coaches and players must develop. I think umpires understand that they are the neutrals, and they understand that emotions are an important part of the game, and it is a competition. If things don't go right, you're going to have some type of reaction. One reason a manager would go on the field is if a player is disputing a call, and you certainly don't want to leave him out there to dispute it by himself. Usually, that's going to go on too long, and it may mean ejection and you lose a player. So you may run out there just to save your player. I think another

MISCELLANEOUS

reason you may want to go out there is that you could have a tough call go against you, and you want to show your team that you're into the ball game, and you care about whatever that outcome was that went against you. If you just sit back and tend to take everything that comes your way, they tend to be lackadaisical and not try to force the issue themselves. However, a word of caution on this issue: What you don't want to do is use the umpires as an excuse for your poor play or your poor managing, and that sometimes happens. A player will make a mistake or a pitcher will make a mistake, and they'll try to blame it on the umpire by shifting the spotlight to them. The manager comes out and just reinforces that – big mistake. Just admit what you did wrong and go on about your business.

JOE BUCK: **Why are there no left-handed catchers, and for that matter, why are there no left-handed middle infielders?**

TONY LA RUSSA: That's an area that's probably easier to answer about the infield part. It's almost impossible to play second base as a left-hander when you think about the double play. A left-handed player cannot make that play without spinning all the way around, and that makes it look so awkward that nobody even tries it. As a shortstop, it's not quite as awkward, but the play in the hole would be something very difficult to make. You just don't see many lightning, range-type guys who throw the ball left-handed. Catching is a different area. There are really few reasons why a catcher couldn't be left-handed. In fact, in Chicago, I had this very gifted defensive player named Mike Squires, a first baseman, who not only caught at times but played third base at times, because he was so gifted at catching the ball and throwing accurately. But catching, here again, there aren't many reasons why you don't do it, but most left-handed throwers become first basemen or outfielders.

MISCELLANEOUS

JOE BUCK: **Tony, players are at the park hours before a game doing a variety of different things. As game time nears, how does a manager focus his team on that night's game?**

TONY LA RUSSA: I think you want to be careful intruding on their early time at the ballpark. If you start pushing and pressing too soon, and you start getting that intensity going too soon, not only are they going to burn out several hours later when the game starts, but they may actually rebel and start staying at the hotel or their homes and come to the park later. You really want to encourage them to come to the ballpark, enjoy the camaraderie that they have with their teammates and get into their routines. They may answer mail; they may look at tapes. They want to get into a routine of getting ready for the game, and you don't want to interrupt it. I think a common way to start paying attention to the game is: Once hitters start hitting, tossing in the cage, or once you go out for batting practice, that's really where you start focusing on the game. You can go up as a manager and you can remind guys, "Well, with today's pitcher, you know, we can run. We can run the hit-and-run more." You can remind your outfielders, "Hey, this is a team, every time they get a base hit they're always trying to round the base, go for extra bases." You can tell your infielders, "This team really likes to push for stolen bases." So I would really try to save that for batting practice, and then you really key into, "Let's really be ready to go when that first pitch is thrown."

JOE BUCK: **Describe a typical day for you. When do you arrive at the ballpark, and what do you do before the game to get ready?**

TONY LA RUSSA: Typically it's a night game, and you try to get there as early in the afternoon as you possibly can. A lot depends on when in the series is the game. For example, if it's the first game of the series, there's an awful lot to do with trying to get ready for that ball club. You are thinking about their offense and their defense. You are thinking about their manager. There are a lot of things in preparation, not just for Tony La Russa but for any of our

MISCELLANEOUS

coaches and our players. As you get into the series, then you start to change, because we try to play a series with an idea of how we're going to score or prevent the scoring. You get to the second day, and you want to re-evaluate what you thought you were doing and how it worked or didn't work. You also want to look back at what you thought as far as strategy; if you thought that you were going to push in a way or not be able to do something. For me, it's like taking a test. If you have studied for the test, you walk into the classroom ready to go. You don't feel pressure; you don't feel apprehensive. You may feel nervous, but you are as prepared as you can be. I think this is the same way for managers or the team. You want to be prepared for the opponent. That means you take a certain amount of time to try to learn about them.

JOE BUCK: Let's talk about charting a game. Why do teams do it, who does it and what are you charting?

TONY LA RUSSA: Great question. More and more of it is being done. Several reasons – some clubs do it just because the guy they use is the next game's pitcher. It is a way for him to pay attention to the game, really focus on the lineup he will face the next night. Normally, what you suffer from doing that is his charting is not as precise as you need if you're going to be a team that uses the charts to base your pitch selection and your defensive positioning. With the Cardinals, we are a very strong charting team. Dave Duncan, in fact, has pioneered charts over his twenty years of coaching that many teams now use. Dunc is an absolute bear about the quality of information that gets put on those charts. The Cardinals actually have a young man named Chad Blair who charts the game. He does it exactly, and it's then followed up the next day. If there is a TV replay, you can be sure Duncan will then look at it a second time to be sure that the information is put in correctly. What we do from that is decide how to pitch guys and where to position our defense.

MISCELLANEOUS

JOE BUCK: **Last year, Brian Jordan hit over .400 in RBI situations. Is that sort of a statistical fluke, or are there some players who just seem to come through in the clutch?**

TONY LA RUSSA: I think what you find is that this is something we all study. What is it? What are the elements of a clutch hitter? Last year, Brian Jordan fit those elements, and I think he will fit those elements again this year, but it's something you can teach and improve hitters as far as their clutch production. What are some of those elements? Most RBI guys, number one, want to be up there with the responsibility of driving in a run. Some guys do not like that spotlight. Secondly, once you're in that situation, you should have an attitude of aggressiveness. You very rarely ever see somebody productive that goes up there and is afraid to swing the bat or consistently gets two strikes before he ever offers at the pitch. You watch Brian, Brian was very ready to swing in those RBI situations. Also, you see a guy who seems to concentrate better with men on base. Sometimes a hitter will drift a little bit, and he may chase pitches with nobody on, like Brian did last year. All of a sudden you put a guy on base, his concentration improves, he's really looking at the pitch, he's trying to get into the strike zone and then he's very aggressive with it.

JOE BUCK: **When a manager or hitting coach is watching a hitter take batting practice, what kind of things is he looking for?**

TONY LA RUSSA: Actually, it depends on whether you are looking at your hitters or their hitters. If you are looking at their hitters, you're really trying to get a feel for the type of hitter he is, if you don't really have a good understanding. In batting practice, very commonly guys will ask the pitcher to throw the ball to areas they like to swing at. You can start to get a feel whether the guy likes the ball up or he likes it down, whether he prefers a ball in or out over the plate. You also see where the majority of his balls are being hit after the first round or two; then he's sufficiently warmed up and that will help you with your defensive positioning. If it's your

MISCELLANEOUS

hitter, we like to have a routine with our hitters. We think it's the best way to get ready for a ball game. So we do certain things about handling the bat, whether it's getting the guy over or whether it's playing hit-and-run. Usually early in the round, you want to try to hit the ball to the opposite field – get you on the ball, get you nice and loose. As you get into your second or third round, then you can start trying to hit more for distance. If it's your hitter, you want to see if he's following the routine that he's taken at batting practice and get an idea that he's not up there trying to pump balls into the seats. Home Run Derby doesn't help you much when the game starts.

JOE BUCK: **Tony, how much of a factor do individual goals play in your decision making process, talking about things like a no-hitter or an iron man streak when the game is on the line?**

TONY LA RUSSA: Obviously, nothing can get in the way of your best chance to win. This is a team game, where you can't get too individually oriented. I tell the players all the time, if you want to be an individual, be a tennis player or a golfer, but in baseball you're a part of a team game that definitely dominates. But I do think, as long as you don't think that it effects your chance to win, you should be aware of what is happening with your players, because the more players get good things going, the more excited they get, and the more they're building on success. For example, last year Royce Clayton was involved in every game for a long time, and there were several times when I wanted to give him a rest, so I made sure that he got an appearance late, just to keep the iron streak up. So, I think the key factor there is, you want to watch the game, you want to be sure that you respect it and honor it, and never let individuals get ahead of team. However, there's nothing wrong with being aware of something that's happening with one of your players. And if you can do both, take care of the team and the great game of baseball and also take care of the player, I think it's a good idea, and it shows players that you have a concern for them. But you also are concerned for the game.

MISCELLANEOUS

JOE BUCK: **Tony, to you, how important is clubhouse harmony for a team to be successful? Does something like that come from the players themselves, or is that something that the manager can have control over?**

TONY LA RUSSA: I always gauge how much I think a guy really knows or a lady, whoever it is that talks about chemistry, and very often I think it's kind of a fad to say, "Well, that's overrated, there isn't anything such as team feeling." I know that, very often, that makes a difference between teams. You cannot live together from spring training to hopefully some time in October without the feeling that exists in the clubhouse being a very important asset or a liability. So we really try to build that kind of feeling. I refer to it as just like adding a superstar to your team, if you have that kind of great vibes between players. Whose responsibility is it? Everybody that's involved with the team, from the top to the bottom: Our club house people, Buddy Bates and the way he does his job, the training staff, the coaches with their attitudes and their care for the players. The manager, obviously, can set a certain tempo, but I really think this is an area where team leadership is needed, and where players have to speak up. There will some times during the season where you'll start to drift in the wrong direction, and the players have to tell each other, "Whoops, that's not the way we want to go." A team feeling is very important for all involved.

JOE BUCK: **Tony, during a game, does the manager make all of the strategic decisions or, like in football, are some of those responsibilities delegated to your individual coaches?**

TONY LA RUSSA: I think that you will find cases in baseball where coaches have some responsibilities. They may have responsibilities for positioning the defense, such as defending the running game, for example; maybe even some of the things offensively like stealing bases. However, I was taught, one of my earliest tutors was Paul Richards, and he told me that every time there's a decision to be made in the game, it's an opportunity for

MISCELLANEOUS

the manager to earn respect and credibility from his team. Plus, he has the ultimate responsibility if the thing goes wrong; he's going to lose his job first. So I think most managers that I've seen, the guys that I think do the best job in both leagues, they make all the decisions. A lot of the preparation, the teaching, and the getting ready, you delegate that, and if you have great coaches, you can ask for opinions during the course of the game. I'll talk to Dave Duncan all the time. How does this guy look to you? Do you think he's losing his stuff? Has he got it? You'll talk to your hitting coach. Who do you think is the best pinch-hitter for this particular situation? I'll talk to Rene Lachemann: Do you think this team is likely to run in this situation? But more than anything, when it's that decision, the manager has to make it, and if you delegate, you're making a big mistake.

JOE BUCK: **Tony, in preparing to play a ball club, do you rely more on charted tendencies or the report of an advance scout?**

TONY LA RUSSA: Good question, and I think it depends on your situation. Obviously, I was in the American League for 16 years, and when you have that kind of mental service going against clubs and those players, managers and coaches for years, you develop a lot of your own charts and information. The advance scout then just supplements or complements what you already have. He'll tell you about a new player or a hot player or something that's different from what you expect. Coming over to St. Louis a couple years ago, I saw so many new players, new parks, new managers, new coaches – the advance scout was much more important. You had to rely on him. What we're doing now two years later, we're trying to build on that body of information that you accumulate yourself. What you want to do is go into a game with an idea of your club against their club. The more that you observe yourself is better, because the scout is watching that club against another team; he's not watching them against your team. They won't pitch to your guys exactly the same. The more you have that information about your team, the better chance you have. Then you just use the advance scout to complement what you feel from the information that you chart yourself.

MISCELLANEOUS

JOE BUCK: Tony, do double-headers present special challenges for a manager?

TONY LA RUSSA: They present special challenges for everybody at the ballpark. Fans sitting through five hours of baseball. For broadcasters, that's a challenge. The whole roster has to deal with it. A major league game is very taxing, exhausting and challenging. You multiply that by two for a double-header. Especially in the '90s version of a day-night double-header, where you're at the ballpark for 16-18 hours. That's really a special kind of agony. However, the challenges, I think, are selecting your starting pitcher. Where is the match-up that gives you the best chance to win? Who pitches in game one? Who pitches in game two? Then it's selecting the line-ups. You get their pitcher against you, and you try to figure out, "All right, we want to win both games." But at the end of the game what you really hope is that you have a roster that's not so fatigued they can't play the next day or next few days – especially your pitching staff. I think that's really the danger you should talk about the most. You have to really guard your pitching staff in a double-header. I've seen and been involved in games where you go through so much pitching that, for days afterwards, your bullpen is depleted, and you pray that you don't have an extra-inning game anywhere in one of those first two games.

JOE BUCK: Tony, I see you, throughout the course of a game, making a lot of notes on a card. Without giving away too much, exactly what are you writing down during the course of the game?

TONY LA RUSSA: There's an idea that was passed along to me early in my managing career, when I went around asking everybody that I knew, "Tell me something about managing." The guys I give the most credit in this particular area are Dick Williams and John McNamara. They told me that, and I found this out to be true, there are two big important reasons. At the end of the night when you're replaying the game, you may be alone. You don't have access to the scorebook; you don't have access to the charts,

MISCELLANEOUS

because you're in the room by yourself or wherever. If you just pull out your line-up card, you have a record of what happened in that game. You can really replay the game, and it gives you a chance to look at your side and their side. You have an awful lot to learn. We go into a game trying to figure out whether we can hit or pitch against a club. The other reason it's so important is that you may not play that same club for six weeks or two months. And when you bring it back, when you try to resurrect what happened in that game against Pedro Martinez, if you can bring up your notes, you'll have a lot of little keys there to say, "Hey, he always threw a fast ball here," or, "We stole on him there." So I try to put notes that either refresh me that night or help me a couple months from now.

JOE BUCK: Tony, as a manager, how important is it to anticipate one or two innings ahead of time, what might happen in a particular ball game?

TONY LA RUSSA: One of the most fun parts of strategizing a game – I think this is one thing that fans enjoy so much – is that you can do the same thing any manager would do. You really are strategizing or looking, if you're playing the first inning, you're actually looking to the seventh, eighth and ninth innings. Maybe not as intently as you are the inning you're playing or a couple ahead. But as far as the question, you're always looking an inning or two, four, five, six or seven ahead. In fact, as you get into the game, you start reducing the innings you're looking ahead. But you should never make a move in the second, third, fourth, or fifth inning and not being aware of what the eighth and ninth is as far as your bullpen, as far as pinch-hitting. You want to be careful how you use your bench. And so the answer, I think, is not only do you try to play the inning that you're involved in right then, not only do you look a couple innings ahead, but you always are aware of seven, eight, nine. That means the only time you get to where you're thinking an inning or two ahead is when you get to the seventh, eighth or ninth because then you're really talking about wanting to have as many bullets in your gun as you can. You want to have your best relievers; you want to have your best pinch

MISCELLANEOUS

hitters. And if you start doing that too early in the game without being aware of the last three innings, you're going to really come up short.

JOE BUCK: Tony, what differences are there in your game strategy when you're playing on the road as opposed to playing at home?

TONY LA RUSSA: Well, I think you always look for the lift from your home fans; the excitement can really be an extra dimension to your ball club. So you look for it at home. It's the same point, though, when you go into a ball park where fans are there and they're loud. You want to make sure your club is mentally tough enough to deal with it. Or if there's nobody coming to the visiting ball park, and it's real quiet, you want to make sure your players don't sleep through the series and not think that it's important. So part of it is just the atmosphere. The other part is that you want to try to look at what's involved in each game and make it a plus. On the road we talk about, "Hey, this is a great opportunity to score first. It's a chance to show the fans in Chicago or Cincinnati, St. Louis Cardinal baseball." At home you want to say, "We're going to have the last at bat. Let's hold them in the top of the first so we can get the lead in the bottom of the first." Then I think you know your home ballpark. Usually you will tailor your roster to match your ballpark. When you get on the road, you're going to have to be aware of the differences in that particular park, and there are differences. You want to alert your team before the game: What is it about this ballpark that makes it tougher to win?

JOE BUCK: Tony, do you agree with the philosophy that when you're one run behind in the late innings, you play to tie at home but to win on the road?

TONY LA RUSSA: I think, generally, my answer would be yes. I think that you're always comfortable playing a tight game, a tie game, when you're at home, because as soon as you get the player and the club out in the ninth, you know you have six outs to win that game. You're going to hit in the bottom of the ninth; you're

MISCELLANEOUS

for sure going to hit in the bottom of the tenth. So I think playing for a tie at home is usually good strategy. Same thing on the road, because the other club always has those extra three outs to try to beat you. You generally would try to be more aggressive and try to win that game before you have to play extra innings. The extra innings always favor the home club. Except, and to me this is where you might change your strategy, when you think that you have a much better ball club, especially a much better bullpen or just a better bullpen than the other club. The club that has the bullpen strength that day usually decides a tie game going into the ninth or extra inning games. If you think you have a better bullpen and a better ball club, which I've had over the years sometime, you're not worried about playing a tie game in the ninth inning, because you think the longer you play the better chance you have to win.

JOE BUCK: *Tony, did you have to change your managing style when you came to the National League, where they tend to manufacture runs, as opposed to the American League, where they slug it out? Or does that completely depend on your personnel?*

TONY LA RUSSA: I think the answer always depends on the type of game that's played. What I was taught is: You watch the game as it develops, and it will send you all kinds of messages about what's going to be your best shot to win. It may be very obvious that runs at a real premium. Then you ought to do everything you can to stop one run. That way, you may be playing the infield in early in the game. It may be the kind of game where runs are easy to come by, and you don't want to give up outs, like you don't want to be sacrificing and giving up one of your precious 27. So, I think the game dictates your strategy. With American League versus National League, in the American League a lot more games are played where runs seem to come in bunches. So your strategy, because it's that type of game, would be to be careful with your outs; maybe push for a bigger inning. In the National League, more games are played where a lot of runs are not scored. Runs are at a premium, so the strategy therefore is try to push wherever you can. Try to manufacture a run here or there and stop every run you can.

MISCELLANEOUS

JOE BUCK: Tony, do you speak with the minor league managers to discuss particular things you want players to work on, or certain ways you want things taught, or is that somebody else's job?

TONY LA RUSSA: That's a matter of communication throughout the organization. With the Cardinals, you have Mike Jorgensen who runs the minor league system. You have Walt Jocketty who runs the major league. Mike and Walt are talking all the time. Tony, the major league manager, would talk to Walt, who would talk to Jorgy. Jorgy then talks to Joe Patini, who talks to Mark Riggins. Walt talks to Joe Pettini, who talks to Mark Riggins. When you send a player from the major leagues to the minor leagues or they come back and forth, it's not uncommon for the manager or the coach to talk to Gaylen Pitts at our AAA, or Chris Maloney at AA. If he's a pitcher, Dave Duncan could talk with the pitching coach, Marty Mason. What I'm trying to say here is you have a lot of people that are involved in the organization, and they all can be talking about a pitcher or player. And normally what you want to try to do is to standardize how the organization plays. That's what's so great about spring training, where you're together and you have a lot of the same bunt defenses and a lot of the same defense against the double steal. So, as far as who talks, I think we all talk. But the guys that really carry the ball are Walt and Mike Jorgensen.

JOE BUCK: Tony, players routinely have various incentive clauses in their contracts. Are you made aware of such contract clauses or is it better for you, the manager, to be unaware of such things?

TONY LA RUSSA: Absolutely it's better if you're not aware. In fact, you can get upset, and I have gotten upset, if a player there in the last month will come up to me and say, "You know, I need so many appearances or so many innings or so many to make this and that." It really upsets you, because what you want to have is a certain integrity to your decisions. That integrity has to be that you're trying to put the best club on the field to win the game all

MISCELLANEOUS

the time. The minute that you start raising any kind of question in anybody's mind – the player's mind or the organization's mind – that you're decisions are being clouded by some type of influence about incentives, it creates all kinds of terrible problems. So I definitely do not want to know anything about incentives. I want to make every decision based on who should play and who should pitch according to what gives the Cardinals their best shot to win. It does come up more now than it used to. You know, incentive contracts and incentives in contracts are a big thing now. It's kind of natural for a player to want to get it across to you. But I definitely try to throw up a barrier. I don't want to know; I don't think it's fair to know.

JOE BUCK: **Tony, what factors do you consider when you decide how many pitchers as opposed to how many position players you'll keep on your active roster?**

TONY LA RUSSA: I think the first consideration is: Where is the quality on your club? If you have better position players and not as many good pitchers, then you may want to add that extra position player to your final makeup. For example, if you've got 15 or 16 very good players. and they can help you win, you might want to go with nine or ten pitchers. If you have a lot of extra pitchers, and you don't really have the extra players that are that good, you want to protect yourself and your pitching staff. Mostly, it comes down to a determination of how many innings do you expect to get from your starters, and I think that's probably the biggest key of all. If you have starting pitching that's kind of vulnerable for talent or for arm stamina, and you know you've got to go to the bullpen early, you need to carry that extra pitcher or two in your bullpen. If you have three or four of your five starting pitchers who will get you deep into the game every time they pitch, then you won't need as many relievers. You can go with 10. I think with the Cardinals this year, we're going with 11 pitchers and 14 players, because we think have some stamina in our rotation.

MISCELLANEOUS

JOE BUCK: Tony, during interleague play, National League teams on the road can use a designated hitter while American League teams on the road cannot. How tough is it to build a team for one style, and then have to use another?

TONY LA RUSSA: It's actually pretty tough. American League clubs almost always will try to have a DH who's a very good offensive player and probably has limitations defensively. So when they have to play in a National League park, that very good hitter – who, as a DH, usually hits somewhere around three to five – that American League DH will not be in their lineup because he is a defensive liability. That hurts the American League club because they set their lineup around this key guy. From the National League side, it's easier, I think, to add a DH from one of your bench guys. But the fact is that the DH is probably not going to be as potent as the American League DH, because on the bench in the National League, you want a guy who can play some defense and get a base hit, and has more versatile skills. So, I think it does create a problem for either side. It probably creates a bigger problem for the American League club, losing the DH and playing the pitcher in the lineup.

JOE BUCK: Tony, how does a team find time to teach its younger players while at the Major League level?

TONY LA RUSSA: Great question that comes up more and more in today's baseball, since so many young players are rushed to the big leagues. I think it depends on what you're teaching. The fact is, if you're trying to teach them basic fundamentals, it's very difficult at the big league level. You can think about bringing them out early for drills, going over basic things. But if you're talking about chasing a ball down, making a double play, throwing to the right base, bunting or anything – it's tough to get that extra work at the big league level, because there's always a distraction. There's a big league game that night, and that's where your concentration's going to be. Teaching players fundamentals is not easy in the big leagues, because you just can't get in that early

MISCELLANEOUS

work like you do in the minor leagues. What you can teach at the big league level is to learn to be a quality winning professional. That's a lot of what happens between your ears – how you handle situations, how you adjust to big league life, traveling, taking care of yourself – that's what winning is all about. You can get that from your teammates, you get that in the clubhouse, you get that around the batting cage. The younger player has a lot to learn, but some of his basic fundamentals should have been taught before he gets there.

JOE BUCK: Tony, do major league managers or coaches try to steal the other team's signs, or is this something that has dwindled over the years? Is this something that was more evident in the game, let's say 20 years ago?

TONY LA RUSSA: I think one of the things that usually gets you a laugh at banquets is when you say it's more important to concentrate on your own team getting your own signs. And people laugh, but that's true. If your club does what you're trying to get them to do by learning your signs, then that's more important. That happens every day. But it's not so much a lost art. I think some teams concentrate on stealing signs more than others. There are a couple of places that you get them. You can try to look at the bench, because the bench has to transmit the sign to the third base coach. Obviously, the third base coach is out there for everybody to watch. Over the years, I've always been fascinated by that part of the game. I've been involved with a few coaches who have really studied it, and two in particular are Charlie Lau and Joe Novsek. They were kind of famous for being able to steal signs. So I've asked them, what do you look for? They've passed along some tips, so I look and our coaches look. It happens, and that's why it's kind of important to be able to have a system that you can change regularly, because that's one way to get beat if the other side knows what you're going to do.

MISCELLANEOUS

JOE BUCK: Tony, we hear about pitchers on rehab assignments pitching in simulated games. What exactly is a simulated game, and what are you hoping to accomplish?

TONY LA RUSSA: The theory with a simulated game is that the pitcher is working against hitters, and he's working as if we were playing in a legitimate competition. By that I mean, the catcher's putting signs down. Normally, the catcher is also the umpire, so they're calling pitches – it's ball one, ball two, strike one, strike two. The hitter does not know what's coming. The hitter goes to bat, and he's trying to compete against the pitcher. Who are the hitters? It depends. Usually it comes within the organization. If it's here in the big leagues during the season, you'll get some of your extra players. If it's in spring training, you'll call down to the minor leagues, and they'll supply the hitters. You may or may not have a defense out there. It really depends on whether the simulated game is for the pitcher or for the hitters. For example, sometimes you'll simulate a game to get your bench players some extra at bats. That means you want to put a defense out there so that you have a feeling of where the ball's hit and whether it's a base hit or not, because you want them to run the bases. Normally, the simulated game for the pitcher is where he's competing against a hitter. You gather some hitters, and the pitcher is really working the counts, the outs, and if he gets three outs, he sits down, then comes back out.

JOE BUCK: Tony, why don't more young utility players learn to catch to give them more job security, meaning the position of catcher?

TONY LA RUSSA: I think that's a great question except I would scratch "young," because most utility players don't go into that role until later in their career. We have Placido Palanco who is doing that with us, but that's because of our circumstance. Placido could be a starter in a different situation. Most times, utility players are guys that have had some experience. I think when it's phrased that way, there's absolutely no reason that they shouldn't learn

MISCELLANEOUS

catching. I think it would be an important plus for them as far as longevity and having value to ball clubs. It would be very important for the ball club to have some protection for that crazy game, when all of a sudden you're out of catchers. Most clubs nowadays are taking two catchers. It's very possible that it comes up. There are sometimes during the game when you'd like to make a move that you think would help your chance to win, but you don't make it because it involves your other catcher. For example, on our team if Eli is on the bench, with his great speed, you may not pinch run him in a situation because you don't want to lose your second catcher. So I think it's really important for a utility guy to do that. Why don't they? It's too tough.

JOE BUCK: Tony, would you and your general manager ever consider trading a strong hitter for an ace pitcher? The question is asked frequently because that ace pitcher is only going to help your ball club once every five days.

TONY LA RUSSA: It really depends on your ball club. What do you need the most? You get beat or you win in both directions. If you are really hurting in the starting rotation, I would definitely trade a star hitter for an ace pitcher. A lot of people have a different philosophy on this, that you would never trade the great position player for a pitcher because he only pitches every five days. But nowadays in baseball, with as much offense as is out there, you have to stop the other club first, and the true ace pitcher, who is so rare, can give you so many benefits. Look at what Pedro Martinez does for Boston. There's no doubt in my mind, I'd take a true ace pitcher and have the rest of the rotation complement him. Why would you not do it? If you have a good rotation but you lack the ace, yet you don't have enough hitting. You can't sacrifice that hitter. So I think you have to look carefully at your situation. If it was just all things being equal, in today's baseball, that ace pitcher does so much for your ball club that I would do it.

MISCELLANEOUS

JOE BUCK: Tony, with all the big money contracts in today's game, is it more difficult to get players now to do things like sacrificing and moving the runner over?

TONY LA RUSSA: I don't know if I would just pick the sacrifice and moving the runner. I think it's more difficult for these guys to appreciate the professionalism of being a quality, major league player who does as many things right and really cares about team play. This is not because these guys are bad guys or brought up wrong; it's just the atmosphere of the times. They're just men; they're not machines. They're a lot like you and I, and if you put any of us in the same circumstance, we could all talk a lot of bologna. However, when we're faced with a lot of money along with generating some statistics, according to human nature we're not going to listen to that corny stuff about how we have to be as good as we can be, you have to play for the team, and you owe something to the fans and the organization. Most guys will look at you a little sideways. That's just the times – kids are that way. I don't mean to be too philosophical, but these players are just people in society. I do think it's a problem nowadays, and the more good guys you have on a club who are playing the game right, the better the chance they have to learn it that way.

JOE BUCK: Tony, players seem to like playing here in St. Louis. How much impact does fan support really have on a team's performance, and does a lack of fan support hurt some other ball clubs?

TONY LA RUSSA: Taking the lack of fan support first, I think it definitely does. If there's not excitement at the park, your 81 home games can be a real drudge. You can psyche yourself up sometimes for individual reasons, for your team or for the team you're playing. But over the course of the season, it's nice to get that extra lift that a lot of people in the stands pulling for your team will give you. Once in a while, you can use it as a cross to bear, such as, "Hey nobody in this town loves us or nobody cares about us, we're going to show them." But that runs out very quickly.

MISCELLANEOUS

What you have here in St. Louis is the opposite. I really believe, with Mark McGwire, his home record is so wonderful, there's no doubt in my mind that Mark is stronger and he's quicker in St. Louis than anyplace else. The reason is: When he just shows up out of that dugout and people start cheering, that jolt of adrenaline that he gets makes him really Superman-like. He's very dangerous other places, but he's unbelievable here in St. Louis. All the other players feed off that. The St. Louis fan, I think, gives players that little extra adrenaline that makes them physically do more than they can in average times. It's quite a plus.

JOE BUCK: Tony, scouting other teams is common, but do you also scout other managers to get a read on their decision-making tendencies?

TONY LA RUSSA: Yes, and I'm being very careful with this answer, because sometimes you'll have a game and someone will say, "Well, how does it feel to match wits with the other manager?" That's not really what you do. It's your team against their team, and you're just trying to strategize how to put your players in the best spot to win a ball game. In preparing for a club, I think it's important to know the other manager as best you can, and there are some tendencies. The obvious one is: How does he use his pitching staff? Is he a guy who usually pushes his starting pitcher? Is he a guy who likes to play percentages out of the bullpen? How does he use his bullpen? Who are the players out there? Who does he go to first and last? So all of those things are important. From the offensive side, it could be equally important to figure out if this manager is very aggressive. In other words, is he going to be trying to steal at any opportunity? Is he going to push a lot of hit-and-runs? Is he a guy who, if he gets behind in a game, he shuts everything down? Or is he a guy who, when he gets behind gets more aggressive? You will see differences in these types of managers. So, if you look at a manager and you see that one guy is more likely to bunt because he's conservative, you can aggressively defend a bunt. If you know a guy is very aggressive with a running game, then you might try to pitchout a little more just to scare them.

MISCELLANEOUS

JOE BUCK: Tony, the last few years there's always been talk about speeding up the game. Is this a problem, and if so, how would you do it without hurting the flow of the game?

TONY LA RUSSA: To me, when I watch a baseball game that I'm not involved with, I get bothered when there are stops in the action. If the action is nice and continual, then even if it's three and a half hours of continuous action, I'm entertained and I'm excited. I would look for the points where everything seems to stop, and there are some things that you can't really change as far as the flow of the game. There's a stop every time you throw over to first base, hold the ball and defend the running game. It can really slow things down. I think one place I would really enforce is the hitter in the batter's box. There's a lot of time being spent by hitters stepping out of the box after every pitch and going through a routine, wasting seconds that become minutes. If I had one place that I would really enforce, I would tell the hitter to get in the box and get back in the box immediately. If they delay any, I'd point to the pitcher to throw it, because you're going to get a strike no matter where you'd throw it. Hitters would respond that way. I think that would be one way that the action would move along better.

JOE BUCK: Tony, what sort of rules are players given when you travel, and are they different from the rules that you give them when you guys are at home?

TONY LA RUSSA: We were talking about this the other day and how this has changed. It used to be, in fact Red Schoendienst was talking about it in days that he played, that you had to wear a coat and tie whenever you left your hotel room. So, if you were going down for breakfast, lunch, dinner, going to the ballpark, you had to wear a coat and tie. He made the point that, in those days, you couldn't get into a nice restaurant unless you had a coat and tie. Nowadays, you may not get into a restaurant if you have tie on. You almost have to wear jeans and an open shirt. So what are the rules that we use? If we're traveling after a day game, then we have a mandatory sport coat rule. You don't have to wear a tie.

MISCELLANEOUS

Sometimes when we travel at night, say we finish a game at 10 o'clock and we're going to get on the plane about midnight, then we wear casual – not messy and ugly, but it's got to be casual. As far as rules on the road for the time you come in, we have curfew. You can't stay out all night. You've got to get back to the hotel and get some rest, and there's a time to come to the ballpark. More than anything else, our rules are certain times to be at the park getting ready for work and some flexible stuff with how you dress.

JOE BUCK: Tony, sometimes managers win one year and are fired the next year. Do managers have that much influence on a team's performance year by year?

TONY LA RUSSA: That's a tough question for me to answer because you feel, as a manager, you have a contribution to make. But you also understand that it's a relatively small contribution. The game is about the players; it's not about the manager. But I don't want to try to pass the buck. For example, if a club underperforms, the manager has a responsibility to get what's there on the field and get the wins that you should get. So, somebody has to receive the blame, and yes, the players have a big part of that. But I don't ever think the manager should say, "Hey, I'm doing a great job, and they just can't play a lick." What happens more than anything else, when you see a manager get fired the year after he wins, is that he has lost respect somewhere. It could be with ownership; it could be with the front office, with the fans, or with the media. But the worst place is if you lose the respect of your players. Then you're not going to last very long. If you survive that one year, you're doomed, because in the end the players are what makes a manager seem to be effective. If they're playing hard, he looks better. If they don't have a clue about what to do, he looks bad. So, I think it's possible to get fired after you win.

MISCELLANEOUS

JOE BUCK: Tony, when we hear players are working on something, when do they do that work during the season? Is there time before each day's game?

TONY LA RUSSA: That's a good question. To explain the difference between players working on things and teams working on things, it's very difficult once the season starts for the team to work on something. That's why spring training becomes so important. Once in a while you can polish something up, but it's almost impossible to put something in new once the season starts for a team. But as far as players working, I mean the game is so demanding over six months. It depends on whether it's defense or offense, where you would like to be and where you are maybe for a week, which can change with one problem or another. Your offense or defense can get a little flat or get a little stale and can get a little funky. The way to get it back, a lot of times, is to work. So most of the time the work is done early. But if you have a day game, you can get to work afterwards, because you have to show up so early to get ready for that day game. You can work after the game. The best time, though, is to work before the game, and it depends – it can be on the field or it can be in the cage if it's an offensive thing. The important part is: It's not just the work, it's the quality of work. Some players go in there and they'll take a lot of BP. It's a waste of time, because they're just repeating the same mistake. The important thing is what you work on and when you work on it.

JOE BUCK: Tony, can you see any advantages if they were to add instant replay to baseball?

TONY LA RUSSA: No. I know that in these sessions of "Ask the Expert" there's a certain amount of time to explain your answer, so I'm going to mess around for a while and see how I can milk this question into something long enough. But the answer is no, I can't. A clutch play in the World Series, should you put it in to get ready for that play? For a key play during the season, do you want to challenge a pitch that was called, or challenge an umpire's call on the bases? I don't see where it makes a lot of sense. I think, and

MISCELLANEOUS

you can take the football example, if you could find a way to have instant replay where the play is not disrupted, then maybe you would consider it. But every time I see instant replay used, everything comes to a stop. Basketball comes to a stop, football comes to a stop, the flow of play and the competition is on pause while somebody checks a machine. I think it's bad business, so I would never go for it in baseball. Even if you could do it instantaneously, I would rather not. Men, not machines, play this game. I like when guys make errors once in a while, because that just shows you how great it is when they make the great plays. If an umpire blows a call once in a while, it shows you how terrific they are when they get most of them right.

JOE BUCK: Tony, what goes on in the clubhouse during a rain delay? How do you keep players fresh and loose?

TONY LA RUSSA: In our clubhouse, sometimes they play ping-pong, they play cards, they watch movies, and they watch a game that's on TV. I think what you want to do, more than anything else, is maybe they take naps – some guys go to sleep if it's a long enough rain delay. The big key to staying fresh is that, when you get the notice that you're getting ready to resume play, you have enough time there to get your body loose and get your mind back into it. For example, one of the worst things – and common sense tells you – if we're going to have an hour and a half rain delay, why don't we go out in the batting cage and keep swinging, keep taking batting practice? By that time, you'll burn out so fast it would be counter-productive. So normally, the rain delays are something that you endure. In the big leagues they've got great tarps, so you're going to play that game sooner or later. Players have a lot of different things that they use to keep themselves occupied. However, when the note comes down and says the game will resume, they key is to try to make it a point for all the coaches and all the trainers to go around to each and every player and make sure they're physically and mentally ready to resume play. Because the game still counts, and nobody's ever going to have a little asterisk if there was a rain delay in the middle of it.

MISCELLANEOUS

JOE BUCK: **Tony, to you, what's the most important thing that a manager brings to his team?**

TONY LA RUSSA: That's a good question. I think I'd have to say several things, because I think managers have a number of responsibilities. I think an attitude is an important part of it. I think when it comes down to the players, if you're playing really well and the manager's acting like everything's the greatest, the players might have a tendency to take it for granted and not ride that winning streak too far. If you're having a tough time and a manager is walking around like he's lost his dog, the players will have a tendency to get depressed. So I think it's very important to stay positive with your attitude, or at least realistic since you can't be positive if you're doing things wrong. I think you have to address mistakes. An important part of managing is to analyze a ball club, and if they're doing something wrong, try to fix it. You want the club to improve as it goes along. If the players are trying hard and playing hard, it's very important to maintain a positive attitude with the club and show a belief in them so they'll rise to your expectations. I think, last but not least, you're expected to contribute some strategy and some decisions. One of the things that a manger is supposed to do is to make decisions and put players in the right position, and the managers that do that help the players. Once you do that, get out of the way and let the boys play.

JOE BUCK: **Tony, if you were hiring a manager, is there a person you would hire regardless of the team, or are some managers better suited to certain types of ball clubs?**

TONY LA RUSSA: A very good question, and I have a couple of answers. I think the managers that I believe do the very best job, whether it's now or in the past, it wouldn't matter the type of team. Those guys can handle any team – young, old, pitching-oriented, offensive-oriented, it makes no difference. In a two-market city where you're the big banana or the second banana, it makes no difference. These guys could manage anywhere. I do believe, though, that there are not a lot of those guys around. I don't think there ever has been. I think there are just a few of those guys

MISCELLANEOUS

around at one time, so it's important to analyze your club. Some managers are better with younger players and really enjoy the teaching side. That same guy may be more intimidated around a bunch of veteran guys who really know how to play. So, if you have a veteran club that knows how to play, it's much better to bring a manager who is more secure in his baseball background, a major league background. He has a confidence about him and understands what veterans have to go through, because he can maybe help shield them from the press or just let them be themselves. So I think there is something to it, but I would go for the guy that could manage either club.

JOE BUCK: Tony, because there are so many things to think about during a game, we often see you in the dugout writing things down on a little blue card. What are you keeping track of on that card?

TONY LA RUSSA: This is interesting because I see a lot of other managers that never make a note, and they must have a lot better memory. Or maybe they're analyzing this game and watching the videotape later so they make their notes later, or maybe they just don't think it's important. I was taught from guys like Dick Williams and Sparky Anderson that your note card can be a real bible that you can review when the game is over. So I keep track of everything that happens during the game. I keep track of our side and their side, the type of at bat they had, the pitch, the count that was out, any game situation that occurs, such as, did they run 1 and 0, did we run 1 and 0, what the pitching changes were. So I make notes about different things that happen in the game. For example, yesterday in one of our games we had a great relay. I'll make a note so we can put it on our highlight film. To me, tracking a game and making notes – just a little brief note; later on you can fill it in –it helps you keep track because it's true that so many things happen during the game. One thing you try to do as a manager is try to stay ahead several innings, because things happen very fast if you just try to go pitch by pitch or inning by inning.

MISCELLANEOUS

JOE BUCK: Tony, with free agency letting veterans move around and expansion forcing younger players to the majors more quickly, is the type of person managing today different from the guys who managed in previous eras?

TONY LA RUSSA: It seems like managers are getting younger. I think part of the reason is that the veterans have seen baseball in a different era and have seen values that they really believed in. Years ago, it was much more important to play team baseball and try to win that year, and try to build your stats that year so that you could make some money the next year. With the advent of multi-year contracts and all the millions of dollars, there are some value changes, and some of the veterans just don't enjoy it. And I don't blame them because I don't enjoy it. However, I think that if you do see a younger manager, there's not a big difference in the teaching. I think the veteran still would enjoy the teaching. I see a Red Schoendienst still enjoy talking hitting with a player, or in field play, a George Kissell. They still love to teach. I just think that, nowadays, with the type of attitude that some of the players have, a younger manager seems to be able to tolerate it better or deal with it better, and I'm not sure it's a good thing.

JOE BUCK: Tony, to you, what's more important: the manager's work during the games like pitching changes, sending up a pinch hitter, hitting and running, or is it your job in the clubhouse and in being around the team in general?

TONY LA RUSSA: I think the answer is: It's all tied for first. By that I mean, I believe that for a team to win every piece contributes. You may have outstanding starting pitching, but if your relief is not good, you lose. So you need starting and you need relieving. You need to catch the ball, and you need to score. It's the same thing with a manager. You better be able to put all those pieces in. If you're a great strategist, you really understand the game and you have the tendency to make great moves. However, you can still lose a lot of games, because you're watching your club make some mistakes and you're not a good teacher, or you don't have a

MISCELLANEOUS

coaching staff that improves the club and gives the guys an idea of how to improve what they're doing wrong. It's the same thing: You may be one of those guys who may be really smart about the game, but have a terrible personality and guys don't want to be around you. Your players are not going to listen to you when you talk. To me, the manager should understand that every piece of that comes together to form the responsibility you have to help your team get to be as good as they can be. When you show up at the ballpark, what you do before the game and after the game, is part of what you're supposed to do, and it's all tied for first place in importance.

JOE BUCK: Tony, how much influence does a manager have on how an organization teaches fundamentals throughout its system?

TONY LA RUSSA: That's a very good question, and I think it really depends on certain things. It depends on an organization and their philosophy. Some organizations believe there's a real separation between development and major league. Some other organizations look at it as being all one, unified. The Cardinals really believe in the Cardinal way to play. It's all basic baseball. It's been taught this way for years, and it's a lot of stuff that I learned other places. I think there isn't a lot that a manager would come in and change for, let's say, the St. Louis Cardinals. For example, a manager says, "Hey, you know I think we should start doing this," and the team has been doing it another way for years. I do believe, though, that you can emphasize certain keys that you think are really important to winning baseball, and you can talk about them within the organization, and that's what we do here. It always seems that whatever the points are, they're legitimate. It's stuff that is agreed on, whether it's the importance of defense or pitching in, how you pitch on different counts or how you run the bases. That's very consistent. I think what you don't want to do is have a manager on a different page, and the only time that usually happens is if the managers are constantly in and out. That's why it's nice to have a little stability once in a while.

MISCELLANEOUS

JOE BUCK: Tony, what do you say to a player you're releasing, and how difficult a part of your job is that?

TONY LA RUSSA: Let me give it to you in a couple of ways. You do have a situation sometimes where the release is very straightforward. You may even have a guy who is not respected in your organization or by your team, and he deserves to be released in a lot of ways, because he's a bad actor and so forth. You just tell the guy, "See you later!" and that's the way it goes. You don't even tell them best of luck, because you don't mean it. If a guy has had a good career, and he's got his memories and his money, then it's just the end of the road, and that's difficult, but you don't feel that bad for him. The very worst case is the guy you really respect but has not had a terrific major league career, because this is talking personal and professional. You're really affecting his life this way, and there's a very good chance in a lot of these cases that, when you release him, he may be out of baseball. What this means to him as far as furthering his life and having to find a different way to make a living, how he's going to face his wife and children and provide for them — that's a very heavy responsibility. In most of the cases, you do respect the people you're talking to, and you know it affects them. It's one of the very toughest things you can do as a manager.

TONY LA RUSSA

Tony La Russa enters the 2002 season — his seventh as manager of the St. Louis Cardinals — as the Major League's career leader in wins (1,827) among active managers and No. 11 on the all-time major league list. La Russa was hired by the Cardinals prior to the 1996 season after managing for 17 years in the American League with Oakland and Chicago. He and Leo Durocher are the only managers in major league history to have 500 or more wins with three different teams. Regarded by his peers as one of the game's top managers, La Russa's honors include Manager of the Year recognition in four seasons, two N.L. Central Division titles, five A.L. Western Division titles, three A.L. pennants and one World Series championship.

A graduate of Florida State University's School of Law in 1978, La Russa passed the bar exam in December 1979, making him one of only five lawyer/managers in baseball history. La Russa, 57, and his wife, Elaine, have two daughters, Bianca Tai and Devon Kai.

He also holds a degree in industrial management from The University of South Florida in Tampa. He is the founder and chairperson of Tony LaRussa's Animal Rescue Foundation (ARF) and is an active member in the Cardinals' community foundation, Cardinals Care.

JOE BUCK

Joe Buck has been recognized as one of baseball's premier play-by-play broadcasters, winning his first Emmy Award in 1999. He serves as lead announcer for FOX Sports' national coverage of Major League Baseball and also has been a key part of FOX Sport's football coverage, where at 25 he was the youngest announcer to call a regulate slate of NFL games on network television.

He has been part of the St. Louis Cardinals' radio and television broadcasting team since 1991. He has broadcast four World Series, and in 1996, at the age of 27, he became the youngest play-by-play announcer to call a World Series since the legendary Vin Scully (25) sat behind the mike during the 1955 Fall Classic. He also is the youngest ever to announce an All-Star Game.

Buck, 32, is a graduate of Indiana University, holding a degree in English with a minor in telecommunications. He and his wife, Ann, have two daughters, Natalie and Trudy.

ACKNOWLEDGEMENTS

Clearly, this book would not have been be possible without the gracious assistance and permission of Tony La Russa and Joe Buck, whose willingness to allow all proceeds from the sale of this book to go to charity speaks as much for their character as their accomplishments speak of their professional abilities.

Dollar-Help would not be available to receive those proceeds were it not for Sister Pat Kelley, C.C.V.I., who organized and led the organization until her tragic death in 1987, and the help of other civic leaders who have donated their time to help the low-income, elderly and handicapped in the St. Louis area keep warm in winter.

The people at Laclede Gas Company deserve special credit — from Chief Executive Officer Doug Yaeger, who supported this project from the beginning, to the many Laclede employees who have asked most of the questions you read in this book. Special mention goes to Rick Hargraves, Director of Corporate Communications, who conceived both the "Ask The Expert" advertising series and this book, Betty Lampitt of the Corporate Communications staff who coordinated the collection and compilation of each year's questions, and to Communications Coordinator Dave Arrow, without whose help this book never would have been published on time.

Karen Carroll, General Manager of KMOX Radio, and her staff at the nation's best sports/talk station played important roles in the continuing development of this project, including Sports Marketing Director Patrick Elsner and Account Executive David Barnett.

The list of those who helped when needed goes on and on, and naming them all would be impossible. The St. Louis Cardinals. The staff at Media Pulse in St. Louis provided transcripts of the broadcast sessions between Joe and Tony. Joe Schall, a life-long Cardinal fan stuck in Cub Country, edited those transcripts with a baseball-knowledgeable eye, and Jenny Cooper helped smooth the spoken word into print. Some others who came to the rescue in the later stages of production include John Sanders and the staff of SWM Inc., John Rawlings of The Sporting News, and the companies whose advertising paid the printing costs of this book (MasterCard International, First American Title of St. Louis, Inc., and Marcone) so that, as always, every dollar contributed to Dollar-Help goes directly to help those in need.

Special thanks goes to a group of students in Dr. Laura Perkins' Public Relations Campaigns Class at Southern Illinois University-Edwardsville — Jimmy Bourne, Brianne Martine, Theresa Lauters, Mindy White and Chris Hargraves — who chose as their class project the coordination of a special-event Opening Day Sale on April 1.

Finally, mention should be made of Tony La Russa's favorite charity, his Animal Rescue Foundation Tony and his wife, Elaine, created in 1991 to address the needs of companion animals. You can learn more about this fine organization by checkings its website at: www.tlr-arf.org